PeopleSavvy

FOR

Sales Professionals

People*Savvy*

FOR Sales Professionals

LEAD THE FIELD. FOUR SECRETS FOR GETTING INSIDE YOUR
PROSPECT'S HEAD AND HEART AND CREATING CUSTOMERS FOR LIFE.

GREGORY STEBBINS, ED.D.

SAVVY BOOKS
Marina del Rey, CA

Author Online!

For information on seminars and for more resources,
visit the PeopleSavvy website at

www.peoplesavvy.com

Published by:
Savvy Books
944 Princeton Drive
Marina del Rey, CA 90292
(310) 827-2115
Email: info@savvybooks.com
Web: http://www.savvybooks.com

ISBN 978-1-887152-10-5

Library of Congress Control Number 2006910938
Library of Congress subject heading: Selling—books

DEDICATION

This book is dedicated to my wife, Jennifer Cayer. Without her kind and gentle prodding, this book might never have seen the light of day. I'm very blessed to have her as both my life partner and business partner and I am grateful for the wonderful creations that we have fashioned over the last two decades.

ACKNOWLEDGMENTS

Few things in life are the accomplishment of a single person. Rather, the contribution of many other people gives life to ideas. This book is no exception. From the first peckings on a computer keyboard more than 10 years ago, through many drafts, and finally during the process of editing and publishing, I have been graced with the encouragement and assistance of many special and talented people.

Special thanks go to Laren Bright, who played a major role in editing my material, providing guidance in envisioning the scope of the project and for sometimes putting words in my mouth that, remarkably, sounded like my words. Penelope Bright brought order and accuracy to the bibliography—no small task. Thank you also goes to Cindy Wilson of Cindy Wilson Design for producing an extraordinarily readable text layout and to Brookes Nohlgren and her ability to find the slightest grammatical error that many of us had missed though we read the manuscript multiple times. Any errors remaining in the book are my total responsibility.

TABLE OF CONTENTS

PREFACE

When I was six years old, my parents enrolled me in a summer day camp. The camp was situated on over 20 acres of land and had only two water fountains. I asked my mother to buy me a small plastic canteen so that I could carry water around with me, because it seemed no matter where I was on the property, the walks to the water fountain were always long.

The first day, I had the canteen at camp the bigger kids started pestering me for water. I told them, "Sure, a nickel a swallow." They paid me the nickel and of course proceeded to drain the canteen and hand it back to me with a big smile. No worries, I would just fill the canteen up again and wait for the next customer.

The second day, I discovered "market positioning." I figured if I stood halfway between the baseball field and the water fountain I would get lots of takers. I did and they paid me.

The third day, the camp counselor confiscated my canteen. When my mother picked me up at the end of the day, the counselor gave her the canteen and told her, "He cannot bring this canteen back with him. What he's doing is bad and wrong."

That seemingly insignificant incident had some very profound repercussions for me. As I grew, I got involved in more and more sales activities, ranging from going door-to-door selling tickets for Boy Scout fund-raisers, selling vitamins while in college, and entering into my first professional sales experience just before graduating from college.

With every successful sale, I felt great...and bad. I knew why I felt great. But why would I feel bad?

One day I was speaking with a friend about this and he helped me trace it back to that camp experience when I was six. What we uncovered was that with every successful sale, there was a very quiet voice whispering to me, "This is wrong and bad." The small experience that took place over 30 years ago helped shape my perception of sales and how people interact with each other in a selling situation. My friend and I spent some time rewiring the experience so that I could objectively look at what I was doing now and how I was doing it, without stumbling over my past. It became quite an adventure.

Part of my quest was to look at sales behavior—my own and those of the people I worked with. Ultimately, this led me to look at buying behavior to see whether the buying and selling behaviors dovetailed or not. What I found was a lot of "or not."

This was a huge "aha" for me because much of what has been written about sales and selling in the last 75 years is based on the experience of the salesperson, not on the person sitting across the table. This has created a one-dimensional perspective.

I also discovered that in the last 40 years there has been much more written on how people buy and the process(es) they use. There has also been a wealth of information published that looks at things like trust, persuasion, influence, behavior in sales situations, motivation, building customer relationships, etc. Yet most of this information was written for scholars and uses heavy, academic language. It wasn't ever intended for or made really accessible to sales professionals. More importantly, much of this information, while academically validated, hasn't been field-tested by real-world people who make a living by selling every day. You and I both know that there is a long distance between theory and practice.

Over 20 years ago, I earned an Ed.D. (Doctorate in Education degree) from Pepperdine University's School of Education and Psychology. I went to school full time and worked full time—in sales—to support myself. To be more effective, what I did was evaluate my sales experience and identify what I thought were the key aspects of it. Then, using my academic training, I focused in on what I considered to be the foundational aspect area of selling—creating deep relationships with my customers.

This led to a period of seven years during which I examined everything I could find about interpersonal psychology. In the bibliography of this book, you'll see a listing of some of that research; the complete bibliography is over 200 pages long. But being book smart and street smart are two entirely different things. The bottom-line question on my mind was: Could I take what I learned in the books and create a system for selling—a clear and workable system that I, and others in the trade we call professional selling, could successfully apply on the street?

For 10 years I worked with a group of sales professionals who willingly acted as guinea pigs. I would develop techniques and tools from my research, test them in the real world, and, if they produced enhanced results, I would share them with the group. Sometimes they would tell me that the tool or technique worked well. At other times they asked if I had been ingesting chemicals that were clouding my judgment. This usually meant that I needed to rework the instructions I gave them.

Some of what I developed I had to abandon because I couldn't figure out how to teach others how to produce the same results I had accomplished. Probably the comment I heard most was that my new resources were simple, but not easy. They did take work to master. (Well, of course they did. If they were obvious, everyone would have discovered them and would have been using them! That's what makes the difference between salespeople and sales professionals.)

Nonetheless, some people in the group did the work to master them and, once mastered, the tools and techniques became part of their unconscious habit patterns. In other words, the sales professionals would go about their day using them, but not really paying much attention to the individual skill.

Over a period of time, my guinea pigs started producing significant results in the form of more sales and larger incomes. So, the next step in the process for me was to take the fundamental skills and start teaching them to larger groups of people who were sales professionals for some of my select clients.

The biggest challenge in this part of the process wasn't in the training. Rather, it was in the implementation. If the management of the company made an effort to ensure application—by implementing the six- to eight-week reinforcement program—the sales professionals would start to show results. Without the follow-up support, and left to their own devices, salespeople would often fall back to their old habit patterns and within 60 days had forgotten most of what they had learned to do. Except for the rare few who took the responsibility to keep moving with the new skills. They consistently started leading the pack in their companies.

So, it is with a voice of encouragement that I tell you that what you will take away from this book is not only assembled from the most current understanding of interpersonal psychology, but has also been tested where it counts the most—on the street. These are solid resources that work. The concepts are simple; the application takes work. However, I guarantee you, they work. My goal in sharing them with you is to help you, the sales professional, become more successful, more effective—in a word, more PeopleSavvy.

INTRODUCTION

Manipulating or Serving?

Caution! This book could ruin your sales career.

You are about to discover some tools, techniques, and resources that can be—*will* be—very seductive.

Why seductive? Because much of what is revealed in this book can be used either for *manipulation* or for *positive influence*. It may appear that manipulation is easier, quicker, less effort. It may be; that's where the seduction lies. And there's no question that manipulation can produce short-term results.

However, anything done with the intention to manipulate is guaranteed to come back and destroy all your work to build a solid, reliable, prosperous, and rewarding sales relationship and career. That's a certainty. It will happen sooner or later.

Positive influence, on the other hand, will produce for you not only a solid and strong foundation for continual sales, but also a working environment in which every sales call you make will be with a person you enjoy. Why? Because positive influence is part of building a relationship of trust, and trust is based on compassion, caring, and a genuine concern for your customer and his or her situation.

When customers really experience you as someone who has their best interests at heart, they will come to trust and rely on you as a valuable ally in their career.

So, if you gain nothing else from this book, take from it the secret that sales is about developing trust by *serving* the people you sell to. And to serve them better than your competitors, *you need to know what they truly need so you can demonstrate—in a way that they can understand—that your product or service will help them achieve their objectives.*

This book has the keys that will show you how to get inside your customers' minds and understand their motivations. And it will reveal to you how to earn their trust and reach them with your sales message in ways that are virtually irresistible.

How you use it is up to you.

1: TRUST

You're feeling pretty good about yourself. You just had a meeting with a new customer and things really clicked. The customer liked you, she heard what you said about your product, and she was favorably impressed. She didn't actually say so; however, you know, based on the connection you felt with her, that you will get the sale.

A week later, you hear through the grapevine that the customer placed her order with your competitor. Your confidence is shaken. How could such a good sales call, with such good rapport, go so bad?

You're about to find out.

How Do You Spell Sales? T-R-U-S-T

At the heart of all positive customer relationships is an intangible quality called *trust*. Over the years, we have examined the concept of trust with hundreds of top producers. As they have looked deeply at their experience, they consistently conclude that lack of trust, more than any other reason, prevents sales from closing.

Knowing how to develop trust is absolutely essential to building a stellar sales career and is the foundation of everything in this book.

While trust means different things to different people, qualities like dependability, loyalty, and honesty are building blocks that encourage a sense of trust.

Most often, we trust someone when we have confidence that they are going to keep their word. **In business terms that translates to trusting another person if we have confidence in their ability to deliver on those promises they make to us *that have positive economic impact for us.*** Economic impact can mean anything from giving the customer a financial edge to making them look good in front of a superior, which may affect their job evaluation. What's more, we have a better shot at establishing trust if a customer believes the relationship with us is going to last over the long term.

Your reputation as a sales professional is a capital asset. Your reputation for being trustworthy (worthy of trust!) is something you build over time with consistent positive performance. However, it can be ruined in an instant with a single negative event: a missed deadline without telling the customer in advance, not delivering on a promise you made to a customer.

Who Will Trust You If You Don't Trust Yourself?

The foundation for earning the authentic trust of others is an innate trust of yourself. This inner trust is a cornerstone for creating customer relationships. Ask yourself, "Do I trust myself?" Now ask yourself, "Do I keep my word with myself?" If both answers are "yes," you have a solid foundation for building trust with others. If you're not keeping your word with yourself, then you may not have a very deep level of self-trust, and that can erode your efforts toward building customer trust.

The skills outlined in this chapter are focused on building trust with the customer. They can also be used to develop greater self-trust. In both cases, you win.

No Trust = No Sales

We've been told that no matter what you do, few customers buy from a person they don't believe to be trustworthy.

If you are untrustworthy, you still might make a sale if you are the only available supplier for a specific product or service and the buyer actually must have it. Or you might get a sale if the buyer is impulsive. You can also temporarily trick someone into making a low- or no-trust sale. However, you cannot build a career on such an unstable foundation. If you want to develop enthusiastic customers, repeat business, and profitable relationships, you must earn your customers' trust.

Trust is expectation, hope, and a sense of being able to predict future events—at least in relation to you and your behavior. Trust is mutual and reciprocal. Creating trust depends on your perception or interpretation of a person or a situation.

With trust comes vulnerability, comfort, willingness to risk, and security. There is also a sense of reliance and confidence.

One of our clients told us, "When I have felt heard and acknowledged, that's when I begin to trust the other person. Being listened to creates a feeling of safety." Another client said that, to him, it is vital to have a non-threatening environment, so trust can only happen when personal (psychological and physical) safety is guaranteed.

As you develop the ability to support these experiences in your prospects, you will gain their trust...and their business.

Rapport vs. Deep Trust

There are two aspects to trust. The first is *rapport* and the second is *deep trust*. **Rapport and deep trust influence the customer in similar ways, yet they are very different in power and influence when it comes to closing the sale.**

You can build rapport very quickly with another individual, whether it's on a customer call, at a cocktail party, or waiting for a bus. And it is possible to persuade another person to buy something from you when there is mutual rapport. However, **if a transaction will have some sort of major economic impact for the person making the buying decision, rapport will not be**

enough to carry the day. If you want to win bigger orders and repeat business, you need to know how to gain deep trust.

The distinction between rapport and deep trust is often missed by inexperienced salespeople. Understanding them both will put you in a stronger position to increase your record of sales successes.

Rapport has three parts: compassion, connection, and credibility. Think of each of these as a building block in the foundation of your successful sales career. With a strong foundation, you can build very successful customer relationships. Without the foundation, the relationships are fragile. Another way of saying this is that with a solid foundation, you can build reliable future sales. With a weak one, future sales are likely to be hit-or-miss.

Deep trust also has three parts: competence, commitment, and consistency. The taller the building, the deeper the foundation required. The greater the economic impact of the sales, the deeper the trust required.

Here's how you lay a solid foundation and build a strong structure for your career as a sales professional—no matter where in your career you are.

Rapport: Compassion

Compassion

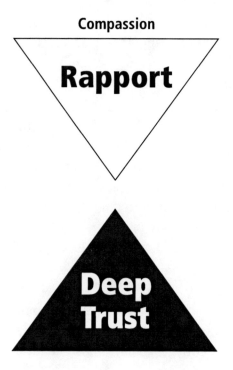

Rapport

Deep
Trust

Why would compassion be a component of rapport, which is in turn a component of trust? Because trust implies that you genuinely care about your customers, their concerns, their challenges, and their goals. Your customer is, after all, another human being with thoughts and feelings.

Why should you care about their feelings? For the most important reason in the world: Because the customer has feelings about *you*. If they don't feel good about you, it will impact their trust in you and will have direct consequences on your sales success.

Developing compassion opens you to greater possibilities. When you think only of yourself (or your sale), your ability to see clearly narrows and you miss opportunities that could otherwise be obvious to you. For example, when visiting a customer and he is distracted, do you notice? Do you keep on making your presentation to a person who is obviously "not home"? Or, do you suggest that he seems to be focused on other things and it might be best to reschedule the presentation for another time? If he agrees to rescheduling, he will remember your being compassionate with him and next visit he'll be much more open to you and your ideas.

Compassion is a process that works chiefly in the unconscious mind. Many sales training books include lessons about how to influence another person. The problem is, the approaches these books offer are generally based on only a superficial understanding of what the process of influence consists of.

Consider that, rather than focusing on influence as the *method*, there is a much stronger influence that is really the *result* of being compassionate. Genuine compassion is a more authentic form of influence. Wherever there is compassion, some influence will naturally be occurring.

How & Why Compassion Works

Have you ever noticed that two people talking together tend to take on each other's gestures, tones of voice, and general physical ways of expressing? It's a fact, and it is quite understandable: According to the principle of compassion, *it is impossible* for two or more people to engage in genuine conversation without approximating each other's mannerisms.

Compassion is a deep state of identification in which one person feels so connected to the other as to temporarily lose their own identity. It is in this profound and somewhat mysterious process that understanding occurs and then influence takes place—not as a manipulation, but as a natural, positive result.

Sometimes, the result of genuine compassion can be surprising.

I met with the VP of marketing for a medium-sized aerospace company to discuss some work they were considering hiring me for. The VP and I hit it off rather quickly and he liked what we were talking about. The president was in the office that day and the VP wanted to bring him into the conversation.

As soon as the president walked in, it was obvious that he would have been happier to be somewhere other than in that room with us. In fact, it was quite clear that he wasn't fully there with us, that something was on his mind.

He sat down without shaking my extended hand and looked down at the floor. So I sat down and looked at the floor and asked him, "What do you want to know about our discussion?" His response was to put his head in his hands.

Here before me was a powerful and successful man, and at the same time a very "feeling" person who was having some great challenges in his life. They could have been business or personal, I didn't know. I saw that my immediate sales job was to be compassionate with him. It wasn't directly about making the sale; it was about establishing rapport so there could possibly be a sale.

Assuming his physical posture, I re-asked the question, "What do you want to know about our discussion?" After an uncomfortably long pause, he started talking about his business. While he talked, I sat perfectly relaxed, letting my eyes focus on the same piece of carpet that his were on. I permitted myself to become absorbed in his story. I was so completely engrossed that I was unconscious of our physical surroundings and was aware only of this man's concern, his quavering voice, and the fascinating human drama he was describing.

He told me how he had created the business and built it up from nothing. During this moment I felt the pride that was in his voice, as though I, myself, was responsible for creating the business. He spoke of the glory years and how it seemed everything he did made money. And as he described this feeling of invincibility, I experienced a euphoric feeling, as though the feeling had been my own.

Then this man spoke of how much the business world had changed in the last two years and how his company was losing contracts. He spoke of how frustrated he was trying to figure out how to make it work. He said that he was looking for a successor to take over his business since his son had shown no interest. I could feel his sense of disappointment with his son as if the boy had been my own son.

As a sales professional, I had become so absorbed in his story that his emotions had temporarily become my emotions. I actually felt his feelings of euphoria and desperation as he succeeded and struggled. In the moment, they became my own experiences.

This partial identification was so real that, when I commented, my voice took on the same hesitant, quavering quality of his. The reality is, in this deep sense *of compassion, he and I were, for all intents and purposes, one person at that moment.*

At the conclusion of the conversation he finally looked up at me, blinked, and extended his hand for a handshake. As he was leaving the room, he told the VP, "This is the first guy you've had in here that really understands our problems." The VP was astonished and wanted to know what I did, as the president never spent more than five minutes with anyone else before leaving the room abruptly.

What I had done was practiced genuine compassion. As a result, not only did I create a positive impression with the president of the company, but I also earned the confidence, leading to trust, of the VP, the individual who would be making the buying decision.

This is the power of compassion. It means entering the private perceptual world of your customer and becoming thoroughly at home in it. It involves being sensitive, moment by moment, to the changing thoughts and feelings that flow through your customer's mind and emotions. It means temporarily living in their life, moving about delicately without making judgments or trying to manipulate. It involves taking on their postures and gestures, not as a technique, but as a means to deepen your understanding of their world.

Why bother to go so deep? Because the more fully you understand your customer, the better you can anticipate and address their needs. And when you address their real needs, you are well on the road to building the kind of relationship that can mean solid, repeat sales.

Compassion begins with unconditional acceptance. To successfully merge with your prospect, you temporarily lay aside your own views and values in order to enter their world without prejudice. In some sense, it also means that you lay aside your agenda. By doing this, real understanding between the two of you can take place. With this understanding, rapport is initiated and the seed of trust is sown.

Your ability to be compassionate is not related to your intelligence or ability to diagnose your customer's problems. Diagnosing your customer's problems without compassion comes off as clinical and cold. With compassion, your prospects open up and begin revealing concerns, hopes, goals, and desires they may never have communicated before. And these will assist you in assisting them, both in their deeper need now and in the long run.

Of course, when customers begin to open up and tell you what's going on with them, you need to know how to listen.

I Know You Heard What You Think I Said

There are many different forms of listening, each producing a different type of response from the customer. For example, most sales professionals are good at fact-oriented listening skills. These skills would include comprehending what the customer's often-superficial needs are and evaluating your company's ability to fulfill those needs. They may or may not serve to establish trust. There is another form of listening, called compassionate listening, that, when genuine, will support the trust-building process.

Compassionate listening integrates an attitude of curiosity. When we listen compassionately, we are fully available and present for the customer. We have no preconceived notions about what's going on with them. We are not busy rehearsing our "pitch" or planning how to respond to what they might say. We are not just waiting for a moment to break in and interrupt. We do not care if we are right and they are wrong. We have no need to defend ourselves or to prove ourselves brilliant, insightful, or witty.

We do have a burning desire to understand the essence of this person in this moment. We are pure awareness, soaking in the words—and going far beyond the words to be in a place of fully resonating with the customer.

Compassionate listening is a way for you to help your customer explore a problem that may not even directly involve you. It is a way of listening and responding to another person that improves mutual understanding and trust. Compassionate listening encourages the surfacing of information and creates a safe environment that is conducive to collaborative problem-solving.

Through compassionate listening, the listener lets the speaker know, "I want to understand your problem and how you feel about it; I am interested in what you are saying and I am not judging you." In so doing, the listener encourages the speaker to express fully—free of interruption, criticism, or being told what to do.

Through the use of compassionate listening, you can influence the sales call by your:

- willingness to let the other parties dominate the discussion
- attentiveness to what is being said
- care not to interrupt
- use of open-ended questions
- sensitivity to the emotions being expressed
- ability to reflect back to the other party both the *substance* and *feelings* being expressed

When you listen well, you:

- acknowledge the customer
- increase the customer's self-esteem and confidence
- communicate to the customer, "You are important" and "I am not judging you"
- gain the customer's cooperation
- reduce stress and tension
- build teamwork
- elicit openness
- accomplish a sharing of ideas and thoughts
- obtain more valid information about the customer and their needs

The bottom line is that you encourage trust.

Premature agreeing, disagreeing, offering solutions, or presenting another point of view can abruptly stop the compassionate listening process. It is essential that you not let your premature opinions block your own ability to fully listen. Suspend agreement or disagreement with your customer as long as possible. Otherwise, you may say something that will stop the continued exploration of your customer's needs.

How do you know when you have ceased to listen compassionately? Here are six signposts:

1. **You start giving advice** or suggesting ways to fix the customer's problem. During the initial stages of rapport –building, you have not established credibility or demonstrated competence. While your solutions may be accurate, they will often fall on deaf ears.

2. **You become impatient.** Your attention drifts and you subtly communicate disinterest. When you realize that you've begun to think about anything other than the person sitting in front of you, you are no longer demonstrating compassionate listening.

3. **You interrupt** the customer and start asking a lot of fact-based questions. There is a time for these types of questions—this isn't it. If you interrupt during this stage of rapport-building, you give the impression that you are "grilling" the customer and you break rapport.

4. **You change the subject** and turn the spotlight onto yourself by relating stories about your company or your successes. Fulfilling your own needs this early in the rapport-building process causes the customer to perceive you as shallow and only interested in yourself—even if your illustrations are relevant to the customer's problem.

5. **You discount the customer's feelings.** Customers may unconsciously share deep feelings, especially when they sense that they are really being listened to. If you find yourself trying to gloss over these feelings by saying, "It's not that bad," or "You'll feel better tomorrow," you risk losing the customer in that moment.

6. **You move into one-upsmanship.** You'll know you're doing this when you start to say, "That's nothing. Listen to this!"

Compassionate listening will carry you a long way on the path to building genuine compassion, and compassion carries tremendous psychological power. It is impossible to accurately sense the perceptual world of another person unless you value that person and their world (i.e., engender compassion). Compassion dissolves separation, allowing your customer to feel valued, cared for, and accepted.

By practicing compassion, several clear, yet powerful, unconscious messages are sent: "You and I have a lot in common. I think like you do. I have needs like yours. I am like you in many important ways. I understand you. You are safe with me." These are the vital messages that support a customer in moving toward greater trust with you.

Rapport: Connection

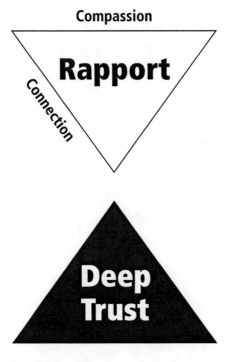

When you first meet another person, your initial decision about them is often based on whether you *think* you like or dislike them. This reaction is generally based on personal bias.

If a stranger walked into the room where you are at this minute, your initial reaction might be based upon such things as their clothes, how attractive they look, or whether they appear to come from a culture that you are comfortable with.

As you were forming your opinion, if this stranger took the trouble to come over and pay you a compliment, you might be inclined to feel more positive about them—though you still know nothing about them.

First impressions are generally superficial and as often wrong as right. Nonetheless, people do tend to judge a book by its cover. No matter how favorable a first impression you make on a customer, eventually you are going to have to provide more concrete reasons why they should continue to like you and want to pursue the business relationship.

With each subsequent encounter, the attraction between you and the person you're dealing with becomes based less upon bias and more upon mutual interests and concerns.

Connecting is something we do well with people who are like us. For people who are not like us, connecting is more difficult, though it is a skill that can be developed. Connecting is absolutely necessary if you ever expect to develop a mutual feeling of trust. Of the many ways to connect with people, two have the most impact. These are *shared experiences* and *mirroring.*

Shared Experiences

When two people have gone through similar experiences, it creates a familiarity between them and plants the seed for a new relationship. Shared experiences may include going to the same college, having children the same age, serving in the same branch of the military, etc.

Janet once met a Senior VP of Sales for a medium-sized company. The introduction was made by the VP of Human Resources. At the start of the meeting it was clear that, for some reason most likely not related to Janet personally, the sales VP would probably have preferred getting a root canal to speaking with Janet.

As she listened, Janet discovered that they had both gone to the same college and had been a year apart. They started talking about the same professors. After 30 minutes of this, the sales VP looked at the HR VP and said, "She's OK. We'll do what she thinks we need." Janet then had about a 30-second conversation on what she would be doing for his sales professionals, and the meeting ended.

The sales VP is still one of her largest clients, and is also a personal friend.

How do you ensure the shared-experience connection happens? It often requires doing some research on the people you'll be meeting with, prior to the actual meeting. The easiest way is to key the person's name into your favorite Internet search engine. Put quotes around the name to ensure that you bring up only people with that exact name.

Internet searches often allow you to gather a significant amount of personal data. For example, you may find out if the person is married, where they live, if they have children or not, etc. The objective of the search is to find connections from shared experiences. Once you've accomplished this, stop. Continuing to uncover more and more information about a person is a form of stalking.

If your Internet search doesn't yield any information, however, you may have to do a little low-tech detective work. You may find that someone in your organization has already worked with the individual and can share what they know with you. Or, if there's someone in the customer's company you know well enough to speak with, they may be able to give you some insights.

As you gather data, you might consider creating a client profile that captures additional information. As you develop a deeper relationship with the customer, they might start sharing more facts about their personal life. As they do, note where you might have a shared experience. This is a natural process for most people; though, as a sales professional, you will be doing this more deliberately.

I highly recommend that you don't tell people that you've created a profile about them. People are extremely sensitive about their privacy, and knowing this can actually get in the way of gaining their trust.

Mirroring

Mirroring involves a very specific way of responding to another person's behavior. It is founded upon two behavioral principles. One is that **our feelings influence our physical expression.** When you are happy, what kind of facial expression do you have? When you are sad, is your facial expression different?

While your feelings influence your expression, the opposite is also true: your expression can influence your feelings. Research suggests that a particular expression modifies the blood flow to the brain and in so doing alters its neurochemistry, which in turn creates the feeling that normally accompanies the expression. If you want to feel happy, put a genuine smile on your face and hold it there for a while and watch what happens with your attitude.

The other principle upon which mirroring is based is called **"reciprocity."** It is a **natural human tendency to return favors.** If I give you something or do something for you, some part of you is likely to feel like you need to return the favor. This "reciprocity urge" is found in every human culture. When you feel you need to give back to someone who has done something for you, you are experiencing this reciprocity urge.

Therefore, **if I mirror your physical expression, I will begin to feel what you are feeling.** If I mirror you in some way, I am actually honoring you. You may not recognize this consciously.

To be effective, mirroring must come from an intention of honoring the other person. If I'm mirroring you because I truly want to feel what you are feeling so that I better understand you, then I'm working to build trust. If I'm mirroring you only to get you to do things my way and am unconcerned about how you feel, then I'm seeking to manipulate you.

The first way, to honor, builds rapport and causes people to feel comfortable with you. The second way, to manipulate, creates the need for the other person to manipulate *you* (as a result of the same principle—reciprocity) and causes people to be uncomfortable with you.

This is not theoretical. It is not, "This *may* happen." It is, "This *will* happen," just as when you drop something, gravity *will* pull it to the ground.

How will people know whether your motivation is one of honoring or manipulation? They may not know it consciously. However, you will definitely see differences in the results over time. In the short run, attempting to manipulate may serve you. In the long run, it will hurt you. Guaranteed.

Mirroring another person's behavior offers them both visible and unconscious pictures of themselves. This is a natural process that most people learn before they are eight years old.

Mirroring Is Not Mimicking

Mirroring is not to be confused with mimicking. Mimicking involves exact duplication of every behavior the other person exhibits. You copy their body movements and other behaviors precisely. Children love to mimic and play this game with their friends. Adults and children will play this game with each other. Adults rarely play this game with other adults except when they want to insult someone. Mimicking another adult will usually destroy trust. So when you are mirroring another person, be selective in what you decide to mirror.

Have some fun with your discovery of mirroring. Go to a popular teen hangout and notice how many of the young adults have adopted the same body postures as each other. Check out other environments, such as the library, video store, or supermarket. You'll be amazed at how people adopt similar body postures and behaviors.

Making Mirroring Work

Mirroring is very simple to do. My first experience with it in a sales process had immediate impact on a major sale. When I first learned about the concept, I was very skeptical. I was told that if I mirrored others, behaved like they behaved, a state of rapport would develop. If I was effective, I could test for rapport by taking the lead, which meant that if I slightly changed my behavior the other person would mirror *me*. For example, if I folded my hands on the table, the other person would soon follow, and so on.

I was presenting a proposal to the vice president of sales for a Fortune 500 company. His assistant was in the room, and while he would not be making the decision for this VP, he could negatively influence it.

We were all sitting in swivel chairs while discussing the various pros and cons of my proposal. At one point, we reached a part that the assistant had disagreement with. His beliefs and my beliefs differed. At that point, he started shaking his head back and forth indicating that he wasn't in agreement and started to verbally raise objections.

The VP noticed this, yet didn't say anything and asked me to continue. I knew I had to do two things: first, state my recommendations clearly; and, second, become more connected to the opinions of the assistant. I did this by mirroring the physical behavior of the assistant until I had established a deep level of rapport.

It's important to understand that I did not try to make his ideas wrong; I simply wanted to establish a connection so he could start to **experience** *my viewpoint as well as his own. As we connected and I could see we were in touch, I gently led him out of the negating behavior, non-verbally.*

What I did was very easy: Every time the assistant started to shake his head "no," I slowly rocked back and forth in my swivel chair, keeping perfect time with his head-shakes, while still making my case verbally. Interestingly, when I got into perfect rhythm with his non-verbal head-shakes, his verbal objections started decreasing.

> *The next step was to start leading him out of the negative behavior. So when I was perfectly matched with him for about 45 seconds, I slowly started to decrease my rocking. I found that if I did this very gradually, he would follow me, trying to keep in perfect sync with me and not break rapport. Was he conscious of this? I can't imagine he would have been. After about 10 minutes he was no longer shaking his head, I had stopped rocking, and he had no more verbal objections.*
>
> *The vice president was pleased with my "explanation" and asked his assistant if he had any further comments. His assistant replied, "No, sounds like a good idea to me. When can we proceed?"*

I want to emphasize that I was not attempting to manipulate the assistant's thinking or argue with him. I was working to establish a connection with this person, honor his point of view with this connection, and present my case in a neutral way that was in sync with him. I respected his point of view and, as we came into greater rapport, he was able to respect mine. The rocking was a way of establishing this connection and assisted us in coming to a place of mutual agreement.

Here are some ways to mirror a person.

Content Mirroring

This form of mirroring is perhaps the one most over-used. Salespeople learn early that when walking into an office they need to do a quick scan and find something that seems important to the individual and ask a question or make a comment about it to "break the ice." This is a form of mirroring interest. Unfortunately, if you are selling to someone who has frequent dealings with salespeople, they may have long ago tired of this "game."

In fact, there are people who intentionally put objects in their office that do not reflect their interests. And remember that some people work in offices that are decorated by others, so their interests may not be reflected in the office decor.

> *A good friend of mine is a crusty old purchasing manager. He's been doing this job for about 35 years. About 10 years ago, he put up a beautiful oil painting of an antique airplane with spectacular art deco lines. The painting recalls a slower, more graceful time.*
>
> *When salespeople call on him, they almost always try to discuss the painting. His response goes something like this: "I hate flying and always get airsick. Now, what is it that you want to sell me?"*

While mirroring shared interests can be an extremely strong rapport-builder, today you need to have more. You need to demonstrate to your prospects that you are interested in them and in helping them achieve goals or overcome obstacles that are inhibiting their success.

Doing your homework before your initial meeting is only the first step. Coming into the meeting, you need to have your eyes wide open, your ears tuned, and your antennae up pulling in the vibes of the office so you can effectively mirror back to the customer.

Notice the environment around you. If there are others involved, what's happening with the people? Are they friendly, cold, or just indifferent? What's on the walls, on the tables, on people's desks? The above example notwithstanding, the fact is that in most cases everything you see gives you clues about who the people are and who they aren't. They just may not automatically be rapport-builders.

With a little practice and enough time in the field, noticing what's missing can give you as many clues as what you do see, hear, and feel. However, as you begin to practice this, just notice. In a later chapter we'll discuss what these things mean and how they reflect what motivates the customer.

For the time being, though, focus on and mirror your customer's unconscious processes.

Voice-Pattern Mirroring

Often your first contact with a prospect is on the phone. Even though you have not physically met the person, and may not know much about them or their company, you can still start the rapport process.

How do you do this? By mirroring the person's voice patterns. Each person has unique characteristics to their voice. Voice-pattern mirroring consists of matching tempo, tone, volume, and accent.

Let's define those terms:

tempo	the rate or speed at which a person talks
tone	the pitch of the voice as it is high or low, or as it rises and falls
volume	the loudness of sound or fullness of tone
accent	the characteristic manner of pronunciation of a language heard in different parts of the same country or different countries

People who grow up in countries where several languages may be spoken develop a natural ability to mirror voice patterns. When they speak with a person from a different country, they may shift automatically into that other person's language. Often they do this unconsciously, meaning they don't think about it and when asked may not even know they made the switch.

Verbal mirroring is something people do naturally. It doesn't take much effort once you have practiced the skill. Becoming more conscious of this skill and using it helps build better connections.

Tempo

The easiest of all of the voice characteristics to match, and the least risky, is tempo. Some people speak quickly, and some slowly. Can you recall a time when you were talking with a person who seemed to take forever to finish a sentence? Do you remember how uncomfortable you felt? Did you feel like you were going to grow old and die before the person completed the sentence? Now, imagine how the other person would feel if you rattled off a sentence back to him at light speed.

Effective connection implies a two-way process—you with the other person and the other person with you. You can help ensure effective connection by being aware of your speaking rate.

The most obvious example of tempo mismatch would be to take a person from the Deep South and put them in a sales meeting in New York City. Unless this person had something extraordinary to offer, they might be quickly dismissed as a country hick. The reverse is true as well; a New Yorker in the Deep South would probably be dismissed as pushy and overbearing because of their verbal speed.

Another aspect of voice tempo is pauses. Some people pause only briefly before starting up again. Others take a longer pause before continuing. Going back to our North versus South example, if you take a short pause in New York, most people will consider that a sign that you have completed your communication and that they are free to jump in. If you're a Southerner in New York, you will feel cut off by people jumping in. On the other hand, if you are a Northerner who starts cutting people off in the South, they will generally consider you rude and ill mannered.

A word of caution is needed here. If your tempo is extremely different from that of the other person, go easy on your voice adjustment. Gradual adjustments to voice tempo accomplish two things. Slowing down or speeding up slightly is not likely to be consciously noticed. Secondly, the other person will unconsciously feel honored that you are making an attempt to connect more effectively with them.

Tone

Tone has two components: *pitch* (i.e., how high or low the voice is) and the *rate of rise and fall*, which indicates attitude. When it comes to the latter, some communication scientists say that almost half of the total communication is delivered through the voice tone. I remember my mother saying, "Don't take that tone of voice with me, young man!" It wasn't the information she was objecting to, it was the attitude of disrespect that was communicated in the tone.

Mirroring a person while on the phone together can be very powerful.

> *One sales professional I coached had a customer who was always "sharp" with him on the phone. He described the quality of the other person's voice in detail and told me that he thought her voice was unpleasant.*

> *I suggested that judging the other person's voice and labeling it as unpleasant was counterproductive. He agreed to work at dropping the judgment and begin mirroring the "sharpness" in her voice. The next time he spoke with his customer, he began to mirror her voice tone.*
>
> *He told me that the customer began to warm up to him and discuss problems that he knew existed, but that she would never admit to before.*

When he told me about this, I suggested two things. First, by mirroring the customer's voice, he initiated and built a better connection with her that she was probably desperate to have. Second, by dropping the judgments he had about her voice, my friend removed some of his own counterproductive thoughts that were blocking him from hearing what she had to say.

Most of us are unaware of our own vocal tone. Because it is subtle, tone is a good medium to use for building connections.

Mirroring pitch can have similarly powerful results in building rapport. Take two tuning forks of the same pitch and strike one so that it begins to vibrate. What happens to the second tuning fork as you move the first closer to it? It begins to vibrate as well. People can be similar in that when you mirror a person's voice tone, you create the same complementary vibration.

When mirroring tone, it's important to stay within your natural tone range. If you sound like a violin and the other person is a bass guitar, you're going to sound phony if you try to exactly match the other person's voice. Drop your voice down to the lowest tone range that you are "comfortable" with. Pay attention; you might notice that the other person raises their voice tone ever so slightly. This is a good sign; reciprocity is kicking in. And, while you're doing this, begin to mirror one or two of the other voice characteristics.

To illustrate how much impact voice tonality can have, consider this:

> *In a recent study, Stanford W. Gregory and Timothy J. Gallagher of Kent State University hypothesized that a certain non-verbal tonality in a person's voice has a profound effect on how they are perceived and accepted by others. In a study that encompassed 30 years of televised presidential debates, the scholars claim that the candidate with better "fundamental frequency"—a subtle, non-verbal hum that is part of the human voice—won the popular vote in every election. The authors link this fundamental frequency to a speaker's dominance or submissiveness.*

While you may not be able to identify this level of subtlety, it's important to be aware of how voice tonality can work for or against your objective.

Volume

Some people roar and others whisper when they talk. If you roar and your customer whispers, it's quite possible that he may feel overpowered. If you whisper and your client roars, you may not gain her respect.

In some parts of the country, it's more natural to speak with a louder volume. In the United States, Texas is a great example. Some Texans just tend to speak louder than people in other parts of the country. I recently overhead two "good-ol' boys" talking at a conference where I was scheduled to speak. While the two of them were standing very close to each other, their voice volume was loud enough for everyone within 20 feet to hear them.

I noticed several people looking at these two guys with daggers coming out of their eyes. While I, too, was a little uncomfortable with this, they were not. In fact, they didn't seem to have any awareness of the impact of their voice volume, just as people on cell phones are often unaware of how loud they're talking, even in a quiet environment.

As a sales professional, you cannot afford to be this unconscious or unconcerned.

If you need to adjust your voice volume with a customer, make these adjustments in your voice volume slowly. If you speak softly one moment and loudly the next, you may actually break connection and diminish rapport.

For some men, voice volume is a marker of personal power. If your customer's voice is louder than yours and he raises his voice louder as you try to mirror the volume, stop raising your volume. You may actually create a shouting match with disastrous consequences. You might slightly raise it again 10 or 15 minutes later. If nothing happens, then it's OK to mirror his voice volume more fully.

Accent

I suggest that sales professionals *not* try to mirror another person's accent. If you grew up in the same place as the other person and you sound like a native, great. However, one of the most painful things to watch is a non-native trying to mirror the local accent and failing. Generally, the locals will view that person as a phony. Think of a person from North Dakota moving to Mississippi and trying to mirror a southern drawl.

Once you've lived in a place long enough, you will eventually begin to mirror the local accent. That is a natural process that happens more or less unconsciously.

Tempo, tone, volume, and accent all focus on vocal connection. Here are some other ways to connect with people.

Corporate Culture Mirroring

Every organization has specific behavior patterns that are acceptable and not acceptable. For example, many companies have a "business casual" dress code, while others require suits and ties. Some companies call people by their first names, and others address each other by their last names. Some companies have a distinct chain of command that limits communication between lower-level employees and senior management. All of these subtle behaviors are part of the overall corporate culture.

Culture, in most organizations, is so much a part of the fabric of the organization that it goes unnoticed by the employees within the culture. What people are very aware of, though, is when someone is not in alignment with the culture.

For most of us, rules such as how we speak or act with each other are different on the job than at home. Imagine speaking with the CEO of your company the way you speak with a younger brother or sister. Would you do it? What would the consequences be for doing it? While these are some of the obvious things, they point out that you must be conscious of the rules of the customer's organization to avoid violating them and possibly destroying your chances of establishing a relationship.

Let's look at some of the observable artifacts that make up corporate culture.

Clothing. Every company has a uniform. It may not be as obvious as those you see in the military; however, it is a uniform nonetheless. Your job is to notice the "corporate uniform." For some corporations, pinstriped suits, white shirts, and wing-tip shoes for men and the same suiting material, white blouse, and sturdy shoes for women are the uniform. For other companies, especially some computer software companies, T-shirts, jeans, and running shoes make up the corporate dress code. White or pinstriped shirt and suspenders has become popular in some organizations.

Dress varies within different parts of the country and even regions within those parts. Dress may even differ within parts of the organization. Consider how the people on the shop floor dress, or those in accounting, or in the computer room. If you interact with any of those folks, what can you do to mirror them? Would they confide their needs, concerns, and predispositions to you if you were overdressed or underdressed compared to them?

When you're dealing with people outside the executive suite, you can still make the sales call dressed in a nice suit. Modify your appearance by removing your jacket, if necessary. If you're out on the shipping dock and working with those people, you may choose to roll up your sleeves partway and loosen your tie. Leave the expensive watch at home if you're not meeting with a person who needs to see that.

The whole purpose behind having an appropriate uniform is providing the other person with clues that you are like them, which helps them connect with you. The less time they spend trying to get comfortable with you, the more time they can be mentally available to build a relationship with you.

Pecking Order. This is a term that is, in fact, based on the social organization of poultry, where the dominant chicken can peck at a lesser-ranked chicken, and the lower-ranked bird must allow it. In companies, it relates to the business hierarchy—things like when a person can speak based on their level of importance inside the corporation or when to use titles or not.

Business Meals. Customs about when to discuss business at a business lunch may differ from region to region and within regions. In some areas, as soon as you sit down is an appropriate time to jump to the matter at hand; in others, you wait until after dessert. In still others, it's not till you are in the car driving from the restaurant that the subject is brought up.

Gift-giving. Customs for giving gifts differ within certain types of organizations. For example, giving gifts to government contractors may actually jeopardize the recipient's employment and your contract as well. Some companies limit the dollar amount of the gift that can be received. For other companies, gifts are an accepted part of doing business. If in doubt, ask.

Asking a question or two before your first meeting may be all you need to prevent embarrassment when it comes to internal—or even unspoken—rules and regulations. "Are there any customs that I need to know about before coming to your office—things that may be different from other offices you have been in?"

Building Connection at the First Meeting

You're about to have your first meeting with a new customer. You've done your homework and know something about the corporate culture. What do you do when you meet the person for the first time? Mirroring their physical expressions and mannerisms can be very powerful and also provide you with a great deal of information about them as a unique person.

It's useful to think of a person's body as divided into two "mirror zones": face and body. This will make it easier for you to grasp and use the following information.

Facial Expressions. The expressions on a person's face can give you great insight into the thoughts and feelings going on inside the person. Research indicates that we learn to read faces by the time we are six months old. We know when Mother and Father are happy, sad, or upset by the looks on their faces.

While expressions are important in revealing moods, our faces can tell much more about us than that. Indeed, some people who have studied faces for a living claim that our characters and dispositions are indicated in the lines of our face. For now, however, just focus on a couple of simple mirroring techniques.

Do you maintain eye contact while speaking with another person? Does that person maintain eye contact with you? In the United States, we generally prefer to look people in the eyes when we talk with them. Generally, we believe that eye contact is a sign of honesty. In many Asian countries, it is a sign of respect to lower one's gaze when addressing an individual of higher status.

If you pay attention to your customer, you will notice that a certain amount of eye contact is comfortable for them. For most people, staring is uncomfortable. When you mirror the eye contact with your customer, keep it natural and don't exceed the amount of time they connect with you.

Body Posture & Movement. For the most part, the way people hold and move their bodies is done unconsciously. This means that people are generally unaware of what their bodies are doing at any given moment. Mirroring this unconscious behavior is one of the most powerful ways to connect with another person.

There have been a great many books, articles, and even videos produced that purport to tell you how to interpret the messages in a person's body posture. While interpreting body language can be helpful, using it as a key to mirroring can be even more powerful.

For example, what is the implication when someone crosses their arms in front of them? The common interpretation is that the person is closed off to anything you might be communicating. While this might be very true, it could also mean that the person is cold, is embarrassed with their extra weight, has a stain on their shirt or blouse, or is just comfortable with that position.

Let's suppose for a moment that a customer is sitting behind her desk with her arms and legs crossed. Is she closed off and resisting? Perhaps. If she is, the absolute worst thing that you can do is try to be more forceful with your communication or to lean forward and become more enthusiastic or charming. If she's really closed off and you do this, what will she do? She'll resist you more.

But by mirroring her body posture, you can discuss your plan with your legs crossed or your arms crossed. If she is, in fact, feeling the need to protect herself, you are subtly communicating your agreement that there may be things in the business environment that are unsafe. It is as if even you need protection from fast-moving changes in the business environment. When your customer feels safer, she will open up and you can naturally follow her. And if she's not feeling unsafe, but has her arms crossed because she's more comfortable that way, you have certainly done no harm in mirroring her.

The point is, you don't need to know *why* she's in that position; you can connect with her, whatever is motivating her posture, through mirroring.

Another customer in the apparently closed-off body position might just be uncomfortable about the way he looks and is afraid that you may be sitting there judging him. Again, you sit in a way very similar to his. Probably not consciously, but unconsciously, he will tend to relax a little bit more because your non-verbal behavior is neither aggressive nor judgmental. Simply put, you have connected with him on an unconscious level.

Think of this as a dance between you and your customer. When dancing, one person leads and the other follows. For the most part, let your customers lead. Your part is to stay in sync with them and they, in turn, will often enjoy the dance.

This skill gets more interesting in group situations. For example, let's say you need to make a presentation to a committee or board. Glance around the table. Are people already mirrored with other people in the room? If they are, you will have a fairly clear direction as to how to posture yourself. If they're not, then what?

> *On one occasion, I noticed that there were two distinct body postures in an executive team meeting. The president and VP of Sales were mirrored. However, the CFO, VP of Human Resources, and VP of Marketing were mirrored with one another but different from the others. Since my presentation was a team-building session, my first question was if there was disagreement among the group.*

Everyone was taken aback. They wanted to know how I knew that they were not in agreement. As I explained what I had noticed, you could see people begin to adjust their body postures. Within about 15 minutes, most of the people in the meeting were sitting in a similar way. And they stayed that way throughout much of the day, which allowed much freer communication and opened the door to resolving the issues.

You actually do these things instinctively. When you want to talk with a little child and you want to connect, do you stand over the child and look down? Or do you stoop to the child's level and start talking with them? When you are interacting with a child, you're much closer to an instinctive level—partly because you don't feel threatened and you're pretty assured that you're in control. Not only that, you are also unconsciously responding to their innocence according to the principle of reciprocity.

With subtlety, you can do the same with adults. For example, I'm over six feet tall. When I'm speaking with a person who is substantially shorter than me, I find a chair to sit in. That way, we're much closer to being eye-to-eye—and seeing eye-to-eye is much more than just a figure of speech.

When you mirror people's body movements, you're mirroring the way they walk, sit, use their hands, gesture, hold themselves, and demonstrate any other physical manifestations of non-verbal communication. Your mirroring needs to be subtle and fluid. Making sudden or sharp movements is likely to break connection with the other person.

Once connection has been established, body mirroring can shift in and out of sync as the conversation flows. This is normal. As long as you feel comfortable, you probably still have connection. If you notice your customer beginning to appear uncomfortable, check your mirroring. If you are not in sync, reestablish posture, and you will likely improve your connection.

Test this with friends or business associates. Initially match their body posture for a couple of minutes and then purposely mismatch their body posture. Notice their reactions and the differences in the flow of the conversation. After this, go back to mirroring and again notice the differences—both in yourself and in their reactions. Most people have reported that when body posture is mirrored, conversations are smoother and more relaxed than when posture is mismatched.

There are over 60,000 different variations of specific body language, many with specific cultural meanings. For example, if I'm in the United States and give you the OK sign, making a circle with my thumb and fingers, no problem. If I go outside of the U.S. culture and do the exact same, there could be a big problem. That sign, in some cultures, conveys a very insulting message.

Interpreting body language can be chancy if you are not well versed in all of the subtle cultural meanings. Even in the United States, you need to understand what culture a person was raised in, which may be different from what their face and features indicate.

Crossover Mirroring

If your customer is constantly shifting his body posture, it might be difficult to follow his lead without being obvious. In that case, you can use crossover mirroring to connect with him. This means you use similar gestures with other parts of your body to match his body movements. For instance:

- If your customer is sitting with crossed legs, you can keep your arms crossed while keeping your feet flat on the floor.
- If your customer has crossed arms, you can cross your wrists, legs, or ankles.
- If he is leaning back on a chair, you might lean to your side.
- If he is sitting with his legs spread apart, you might sit with your arms wide open.

Subtlety is the key with any mirroring technique. If you're clumsy with this, your customer may become annoyed or ask what you are doing.

Mirroring Emotions

Have you ever had a meeting with a customer and noticed that she was in a gloomy mood? If the two of you had a good relationship, you may have asked her what was happening. She may have told you, sometimes in more detail than you wanted. The worst thing you can do is be Mr. Sunshine and make casual remarks like, "Boy, you look down!" "Did your dog just die?" "Who kicked you around today?" These will only create separation, and you will lose rapport quickly.

Mirroring the person's emotional state is a sign of respect and allows you to more deeply sense what is happening with your customer. Acceptance and neutrality can be your greatest assets in mirroring difficult, emotionally charged situations.

Accepting the person's emotional state will prevent you from getting defensive (especially if he appears to be angry with *you*). Keep in mind that acceptance and agreement are different. You may not agree that your customer has a right to explode; however, you can accept that people sometimes do this—and he just did. Getting angry with him will usually escalate the situation.

Responding in a kind, soothing voice—treating him like he had a recent frontal lobotomy—also often worsens the situation. It only comes across as being offensive or patronizing.

So, what *can* you do? You can accept his emotional position and begin to use your voice tone and tempo mirroring skills. He's probably talking very fast, so mirror his voice tempo. His tone is sharp, perhaps harsh, and you can mirror that. His voice volume may be rather loud; we recommend *not* mirroring that. What you also want to avoid doing is mirroring his content, especially if he is questioning your genetic heritage or speculating on the marital status of your parents at the time of your birth.

By mirroring without anger and with acceptance, you can reestablish connection with him. Sometimes this will be enough for the person to stop and become more civil. Other times, you will have to mirror for about five minutes and then gradually slow your tempo and soften your tone. If you have succeeded in connecting with him, he will follow your lead.

I know that this goes against everything most people ever heard about how to handle angry people. The key thing here is that this *works* and works well, especially if you maintain your neutrality and accept the person attacking you as another member of the human race.

When you emotionally connect, you may be surprised at the depth and quality of information people share with you. Often the person may not even know what he is sharing because the information is coming from an unconscious level.

By using emotional mirroring, you step into the other person's reality—into their world—and you start to see, feel, and hear things from that perspective. This, in turn, helps you adjust your sales approach to more closely match the client's needs and preferences. Consequently, your acceptance of who they are is mirrored as well.

Connecting It All Together

This section has presented to you a number of ways to connect with an individual. Once again, I suggest that you try this with friends and family first. Initially, you might be a little uncomfortable with these skills. Take the time to become comfortable in a non-sales situation. They'll pay big dividends when you've learned to use them well.

There is no need to use all of the connecting skills at the same time. Use whatever skill you need to connect with the other person. Then use the other skills to enhance or deepen the connection. Keep it simple and, before long, you'll notice that people are feeling more and more comfortable with you—and that will open many new doors to serving them more successfully and gaining more business.

Rapport: Credibility

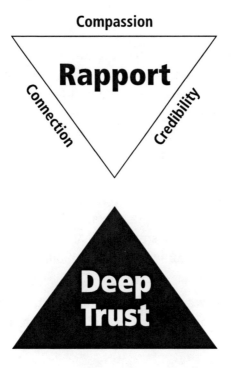

Compassion

Rapport

Connection

Credibility

Deep Trust

How do you get people to *know* you can do what you say you can do? In some professions there is implied credibility because, in order to be licensed, a certain level of skill has to be demonstrated. Not so in sales. With a few exceptions, sales professionals do not have a government-controlled board of examiners to determine if those in the profession are qualified to sell. Even in professions that are regulated to some extent, such as real estate, banking, or securities brokering, the examiners are less concerned with the level of skill in selling than they are with adherence to ethics or legal guidelines.

Most other professionals—physicians, for example—must pass rigorous academic requirements before being licensed to practice. In addition, they have additional annual continuing education requirements that need to be met to be able to continue working in their profession.

Because physicians are perceived to know their field thanks to this licensing, they automatically have a certain level of professional credibility. Because of this, patients will generally follow the course of treatment their physician recommends. They may occasionally get a second opinion, but they normally have high levels of trust in their physicians.

In sales, you can print up a business card, declare yourself a salesperson, and start attempting to sell. There is no inherent trust that goes with being a sales professional since the perception is that anyone can do it. So you must *build* credibility from the ground up.

Men and women who bring value and solutions to their customers are more than salespeople; they are true sales professionals.

They are knowledgeable about both what they sell and what the customer requires.

They are alert to changes that affect both.

They are attuned to the customer—his employees, his practices, and his problems—and are skilled in interpreting what they hear or learn.

They communicate back to responsible plant, office, or management people the information that they have gathered—the unpleasant as well as the pleasant.

They are catalysts who bring the resources of the company they represent to provide solutions to the appropriate buying influences that specify, use, or otherwise affect purchasing decisions.

And **they see selling as a function that enhances the success of their customers.**

But how does the customer know that he is dealing with a professional? By the individual's track record. Yet how is a customer to know what a salesperson's past performance has been? How can the customer differentiate among several salespeople, all supplying the same items? Are the customer's definitions of "performance" clear enough to know what they're measuring? Can the customer capture data that realistically reflect the "performance" he wishes to measure? Does he have reliable systems that enable him to update, analyze, and report "performance results"?

On the other side, do you know and understand how you are being measured? It will serve you to know these things, if you are to build credibility with a customer.

Credibility refers to your ability to present yourself as a sales professional who has something—generally, more than just a product or service—to offer the customer. When you demonstrate credibility, the customer sees you as possessing a breadth of knowledge, depth of insight, and length of experience that may help her come to grips with some of the contradictions, complexities, and dilemmas in operating her business. There are several ways to gain credibility with your customer.

Earned Credibility

Credibility is ultimately something that you earn with the customer. It's developed over time and often requires face-to-face meetings. Knowledge, insight, and experience are the three key elements of credibility.

Knowledge, in this context, refers to what you know about the customer and his business. Doing your homework on the company before you have your first meeting is the price of entry in today's sales game. You need to know what the customer's company is about, who they do business with, what their issues are, where they have failed, how profitable they are, and other information like this. Can you answer these questions about your customer?

- Is the customer's industry and/or customer base stable or evolving?
- Who are the customer's competitors or collaborators?
- What is the customer's competitive advantage?
- What has contributed to past successes for the customer?
- What products or services contributed most to this success?
- What innovations are anticipated that could change the character of the customer's environment?
- Are there any new management initiatives or procedures that will be instituted by the customer's organization?
- How will the future regulatory, legislative, or political environment affect organization performance?

This is just a small sample of the kinds of questions you may want to ask yourself when doing background research on your customer in order to be in the strongest position to demonstrate your insight.

Insight refers to how your product or service will help the customer to be more successful. It's not enough to know the features and benefits of your product or service. You need to have the insight into how those features and benefits are going to apply specifically to the customer's company and help accelerate customer success.

Have you solved another company's problems? Have you helped another company to be more successful? Are you willing to take the time to see if the customer really needs what you're offering at this time? Think of the company as a human being. If a person were dying because of arterial bleeding, trying to sell him on a vitamin regimen to help with iron deficiency wouldn't be appropriate.

Jean, a sales professional I know, does extensive research on each of his customers. He wants to know what the company is about, so he reads the annual reports and the various press releases the company sends out. He ferrets out information about the company on the Internet.

For his particular service, he wants to see if the benefits it offers are perceived as benefits from the customer's perspective. More importantly, he wants to know *how* his services benefit each unique customer. He meets with the customer only after he is certain he has a good grasp of this information so he can use this knowledge to gain credibility in their eyes.

Experience is a little harder to communicate. So Jean has developed a "secret weapon" to demonstrate his experience. Over the years, he has been diligent about getting signed testimonial letters from his customers. After 20 years in business, he now has a binder three inches thick with customers praising him for solving some of their more sticky issues. He always has this with him, even after the first meeting.

What we say as salespeople may be suspect in the eyes of the customer. However, if one of our customers says it, or in Jean's case, several hundred customers say it, it must be true. Jean says that after sharing his binder of testimonials, his customers rarely have doubts about his experience or his credibility.

Credibility by Referral

What if you don't have 20 years of experience and a three-inch thick binder of customer testimonials? You can accomplish something similar by having one of your satisfied customers refer you to one of their friends or associates. Their providing you with a letter of introduction, or a phone call from them, arms you with a modest amount of credibility when you walk in the door.

Even with this introduction, to earn credibility you still need the *knowledge* and *insight* about the person and company you're meeting with. If you take the meeting without these, you risk losing the credibility that has been bestowed on you by the referral. In other words, you are given a certain amount of capital to spend with the new client. You do *not* want to squander it by being ill prepared.

A word of caution: *If you have credibility by referral and do something to cause the prospective client to not trust you, it is a given that you won't be able to develop trust with them. What's worse is that the loss of referred credibility will also impact the relationship of the person providing the referral.* Asking for a referral is not something to be done lightly. People are appropriately very sensitive about making referrals and having them go sour. When you receive a referral, you take on the obligation of performing well, not just for yourself, but also for your client who has referred you.

Credibility by Association

There is one final way to gain credibility. If you represent a product or service that's highly regarded or you represent a well-known company that has extensive industry credibility, you will be given more professional courtesy during the initial sales meeting. The credibility of the company and/or its products and services has been transferred to you.

If you gain credibility through referral or by association, ultimately you still need to transform that into earned credibility. Credibility by referral or association is like having a co-signer on a personal loan. Eventually, the bank or credit union needs to know that you can pay the loan off yourself.

These sorts of bestowed credibility get you into the game. Staying in the game and prospering is up to you.

Wrapping Up Rapport

After reading this section, you may be wondering how you will be able to remember to do all of this while you are trying to conduct a reasonably coherent sales call. There is a simple solution— develop the habit of mirroring.

Rapport is not mechanical. Nor is it as simple as it may seem to those of you who have always set it up intuitively. However, as you practice these techniques, establishing and maintaining rapport will become more natural and automatic.

Maintaining rapport is a way to synchronize with the different experiences and meanings of other human beings. Mirroring accentuates similarities and plays down differences so that understanding and rapport between people increases.

Some people may feel it is unfair to utilize a natural phenomenon such as this to gain your desired-end-result. Remember that you will not gain and retain your own desired goal unless you keep the customer's desired-end-result in mind. By doing this, rapport becomes a tool to benefit both of you.

Taking Rapport on the Road

Now that you are conscious of compassion, connection, and credibility as the three critical elements of building rapport, notice how you are able to implement them within your workaday environment. The suggestion here is to improve any of these skills by doing them one at a time. Make it bite-size. Start with the one that interests you the most or that you find the easiest. Many people find mirroring posture or voice pattern to be a very good starting point.

In work, family, and social situations, continually try meeting people where they are. Notice how they relax when you seem to be in their rhythm. Become aware of how easy it is, once you are in true rhythm with them, to make very subtle changes and bring them into true rhythm with you. Practice, experiment, and enjoy.

Deep Trust: Crossing the Belief Threshold

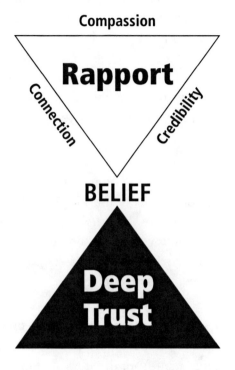

The second primary element in establishing trust is *deep trust.* Where rapport can get the car started, engine revving, deep trust is what gets you in gear and really moving down the road to bigger sales and repeat business.

Your customer brings to the table certain opinions about working with salespeople. She also has had experiences working with salespeople that form the basis for her beliefs. Opinions, beliefs, and knowledge are very similar, varying mostly in the degree of confidence the holder has in them. Knowledge would rank as the most certain, and opinions as the least certain.

For example, if you have an opinion about something and you collect enough evidence that supports the opinion, you transform the opinion into a belief. At this point, you pass the belief to the unconscious and put it into the "how the world works" file. You do this because it frees your mind to focus on other things. For the vast majority of people, this is an automatic process—and thank goodness for that, because you wouldn't make much progress in life if you had to constantly reevaluate every detail of your life.

For example, how much would you get done if you had to relearn how to turn on the shower every morning? Have you ever traveled and found that the shower in the hotel worked differently from yours at home? Did it take you a few moments to figure it out? New facts or new knowledge may require us to reevaluate our beliefs and make changes to our behavior.

Your customer does a similar thing with salespeople. She takes all of this input, both from the past and present, and constructs a mental and emotional map from the information about salespeople found in her unconscious "how salespeople work" file. The information she draws on influences her behaviors in a selling situation.

Does your customer generally believe that all salespeople are honest and can be trusted, or does she believe that all salespeople are for the most part self-serving, interested only in making the sale, and need to be watched like a hawk? Or is she neutral? Whatever she thinks, if her beliefs have been reinforced over time she will be very confident that they are accurate.

Her confidence in her beliefs about salespeople serves as a psychological gatekeeper of sorts, systematically determining how your actions match her beliefs. The degree of confidence she has in her beliefs is determined by the consistency of salespeople's behaviors that match her beliefs. If, in her experience, most salespeople act as she believes they will, she possesses sound evidence for those beliefs. Sound evidence, in turn, implies accuracy. Highly confident beliefs should therefore be highly accurate.

But are they? **There is surprisingly little psychological research that supports the idea that confidence is closely tied to accuracy.** Instead, confidence and accuracy often seem to be disconnected.

The Confidence/Accuracy (Dis)Connection

Some of the most direct evidence for the confidence–accuracy disconnection comes from studies in which psychologists grew progressively more confident in their impressions of clients while the accuracy of their impressions remained low.

Other studies of eyewitness testimony have revealed virtually no relation between the observer's confidence and the accuracy of their observations and thus beliefs. Even when people make judgments about "objective facts," there seems to be little relation between their confidence in their information and the accuracy of their beliefs.

If you want an experience of this, consider these two questions: Who invented the airplane? Who invented the automobile? Did you say the Wright brothers and Henry Ford?

Many people confidently believe that the Wright brothers invented the airplane. But, in fact, there were a number of airplanes in their day. The Wright brothers innovated a method of steering that made flying practical. Similarly, there were a variety of autos when Henry Ford came up with the idea of the assembly line, which is what really put Ford on the map.

The customer's confidence acts as a form of self-fulfilling prophecy. She sees, hears, and feels what she wants based on her beliefs, not based on the evidence that is present. If you are going to move from rapport to deep trust, you need to cross this Belief Threshold. This crossing needs to be handled delicately and may take time, depending on her beliefs about salespeople and their trustworthiness.

In the process of crossing the threshold and moving toward deep trust, the customer will evaluate you on three criteria:

- First, she will try to determine how competent you are.
- Second, she will try to determine if you are committed to her desired-end-results.
- And finally, she will want to know how consistent you are.

Her evaluation will be based solely on your repeated *behaviors.* Verbally declaring that you are competent, committed, and consistent won't have any credibility with her. You must make certain that your actions continually support these three criteria, if you want to cross the Belief Threshold. And crossing the Belief Threshold is a critical step to creating deep trust and a successful and enduring customer relationship.

Deep Trust: Competence

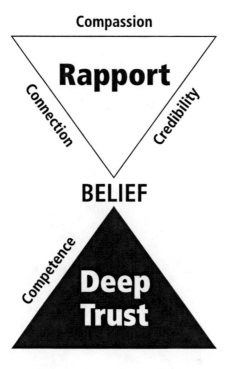

You can have credibility with your clients by demonstrating knowledge, expressing insight, and having experience. Credibility will help you build rapport. However, to begin to establish deep trust, you must be perceived by your customer as being competent (i.e., demonstrating competencies). Competencies are the *attributes, skills,* and *knowledge* considered critical for successful sales performance.

Attributes are the personal qualities in your psychological makeup that contribute to your overall sales success. These include your values, which were hardwired in you before you were eight years old. For example, drive is something that is hardwired in people. If a person doesn't have it by the age of about 21, only rarely will they develop it in later life. In adulthood, it often takes a significant emotional event to create the desire to change and follow through with the change.

Skills are your demonstrated expertise. These can be developed or acquired through training or experience. Negotiation skill is an example of that. Learning to negotiate well takes education and practice.

Knowledge, in this context, is a given body of factual information. That is, it is information that is objectively proven reliable. For example, the specifications of your product or service would be part of your body of knowledge. Deeper knowledge would be how your product or service is going to benefit the customer based on your experience in situations similar to that of your customer.

Here are some specific sales competencies.

Attributes:
- Adaptability
- Drive
- Initiative
- Tenacity

Skills:
- Account management
- Listening
- Presentation
- Interpersonal relationship
- Leadership
- Prospecting
- Time management

Knowledge:
- Company mission and vision
- Competitive strategies
- Financial
- Marketing
- Pricing

Each competency has specific behaviors that identify whether or not you are, in fact, competent. For example, these are the behaviors associated with Organizing Skills:

- Sets clearly defined and attainable goals
- Creates detailed plans that focus on accomplishing goals
- Creates and completes effective to-do lists that track progress toward goal completion
- Uses either manual or computer-based time management systems
- Organizes paper using in-baskets, tickler files, or general filing systems
- Commits to and honors time deadlines

As you develop competency, you go through five stages. They are: unconscious incompetence, conscious incompetence, conscious competence, unconscious competence, and mastery (sometimes called "reflective competence"). This applies for every skill and the knowledge that needs to be developed to be an effective top-producing sales professional.

You may have different competence levels with different skills. You could be a great listener but fail when you have to make a persuasive presentation. You may be strong in making presentations but be weak in the time management area. Your strengths may not offset your weaknesses, and your customer may or may not be willing to work with you when you are at the lower levels of competence.

You don't have to be perfect at everything; however, you will want to bring your weaker skills up to an acceptable level. Knowing which skills are at which level of competency will assist you in doing just that.

Unconscious Incompetence

When you are functioning at the unconscious incompetence level, you probably are blissfully unaware that your confidence exceeds your ability. Basically, you don't know that there is anything to learn. You may not understand advice given to you because you haven't begun to ask the right questions.

And yet you may still be successful at this level. It's called "beginner's luck." You know so little that all you can do is ask questions of the customer. The customer respects that you're interested in him and his needs and awards you the business because you didn't try to pull any fancy sales moves on him. This confidence in you will not persist, however, and you will not find yourself in a solid position over time unless you move out of this level.

Unconscious Incompetents would demonstrate these behaviors:

- They are not aware of the existence or relevance of the skill area.
- They are not aware that they have a particular deficiency in the area concerned.
- They might deny the relevance or usefulness of the skill.
- They must become conscious of their incompetence before development of the new skill or learning can begin.

The aim of the trainee or learner who is at this stage is to move into the "conscious incompetence" stage by demonstrating the new skill or ability. The trainer or teacher starts this process by communicating or demonstrating the benefit that the skill will bring to the person's effectiveness.

An awakening needs to occur to get to the next level. Losing a large sale is often what accomplishes this.

Conscious Incompetence

The awakening event that takes place causing a mental shift to this level may feel like being hit with a brick. You think you're doing great and, suddenly, out of nowhere, you lose the sale or otherwise have evidence that you entirely missed something. When this happens, it may even seem to you that you actually know nothing and that there's so much to learn. In fact, your confidence may drop as you realize that your ability is limited and that you will need to study to learn.

Often this means not succeeding at first. In our culture, people have a difficult time at this level because they label the learning "failure." The good news is that, when this occurs, **you are actually way ahead of where you were before it took place because you now know what you don't know and can do something about it.** So you begin to study.

Conscious Incompetents would demonstrate these behaviors:

- They become aware of the existence and relevance of the skill.
- They are therefore also aware of their deficiency in this area, ideally by having attempted or tried to use the skill.
- They realize that by improving their skill or ability in this area, their effectiveness will improve.
- Ideally, they have a measure of the extent of their deficiency in the relevant skill and a measure of what level of skill is required for their own competence.

- If they want to shift this, they make a commitment to learn and practice the new skill and to move to the "conscious competence" stage.

There are three keys to getting to the next level: Practice. Practice. Practice.

Conscious Competence

Once you've practiced enough and acquired more skill, you become consciously competent. Conscious Competents have the knowledge to perform particular skills, have extensively trained at performing the skills, and are proficient at the skills. However, the skills do not yet come automatically; they still require conscious thought to be performed correctly. Your conscious mind can only cope with a small number of new bits of information at any one time. While your confidence increases with your ability, you still have to concentrate on what you know and how you do it.

Conscious Competents would demonstrate these behaviors:

- They can perform the skill reliably at will.
- They still need to concentrate and think in order to perform the skill.
- They can perform the skill without assistance.
- They will not reliably perform the skill unless thinking about it (i.e., the skill is not yet "second nature" or "automatic").
- They should be able to demonstrate the skill to another, but are unlikely to be able to teach it well to another person.
- They should ideally continue to practice the new skill and, if appropriate, commit to becoming "unconsciously competent" at the new skill.

For a person to reach the next level, the skills and knowledge are practiced enough that they become habits.

Unconscious Competence

At this stage, you can do the skill while your mind is on other things. Your skill has become instinctive. Your confidence and ability have peaked; you no longer have to concentrate on what you know/do. This is the start of the next learning curve.

Unconscious Competents would demonstrate these behaviors:

- They become so practiced that the skill enters the unconscious parts of the brain (i.e., it becomes "second nature"). Common examples are driving, sports activities, typing, manual dexterity tasks, listening, and communicating.
- They can perform certain skills while doing something else—for example, knitting while watching TV.
- They might now be able to instruct others in the skill concerned; although after some time of being unconsciously competent, the person may actually have difficulty explaining exactly how they do it because the skill has become largely instinctual.

Reaching this level and displaying these behaviors arguably gives rise to the need for long-standing unconscious competence to be checked periodically against new standards.

As effective as this level is, there is still one more level to go.

Mastery

The fifth stage is mastery, or what is sometimes referred to as reflective competence. At this stage, you are aware of your own levels of competence and you recognize that, unlike conscious competence, you don't need to think about the skills in order to execute them well. In some ways, it's almost like you're observing yourself from outside of yourself. These won't be the exact same skills and knowledge that you learned consciously and then became unconscious of. It will appear as a flow, where you pick part of one skill and combine it with some knowledge to create a new approach that is totally appropriate for your customer at that moment in time.

The Critical Importance of Competence

Whether they see it through your performance or not, customers know unconsciously whether you are competent. Their unconscious level controls their deep emotional satisfaction, or dissatisfaction. If you do something unhelpful (i.e., in some way incompetent), their unconscious knows it.

The tricky part is that the unconscious and conscious mind can disagree. Your customer may have all the facts to make a decision in your favor, but something you've done holds them back from trusting the facts in front of them. This is why demonstrating competence is so important.

Demonstrating competence allows you to create a safe space within the customer's unconscious. This is the important emotional or interpersonal environment where every detail of your interaction with the customer must reflect safety and support, if you are to build deep trust.

Over the last 30 years, customers have become much more sales savvy. Many purchasing agents take the same public sales training courses as salespeople. One individual I know has a box with every standard close written down on three-by-five cards. When he's meeting with a new salesperson and she uses one of the standard closes, he opens the box, takes out the card, slides it across the table, and tells her, "That's one; you have one more chance."

He's not doing this to be mean. He just doesn't have time for salespeople who are going to be using all of the old sales techniques that have been used for the last 100 years. He wants to work with sales professionals who are competent and are interested in helping him be successful.

Demonstrating Competence

If you had a doctor's appointment and the doctor met you at the door and greeted you by name, you might be very impressed. If he then showed you to a small reading room and pointed out the medical reference books and said, "Look through these. When you've discovered what your symptoms mean, come to my office and I'll write the appropriate prescription for you. Oh, by the way, we're having a special on kidney transplants this week."

How would you feel about the physician? What would you do next?

Requiring the customer to diagnose their own problem is not professional selling. And prescription before diagnosis is medical malpractice. It is also sales malpractice. Yet this is the way many salespeople try to sell. They push product or service brochures across the desk hoping that something will catch the customer's eye. They don't do a thorough diagnosis. **Competence is demonstrated by the quality of questions you ask.**

Demonstrating Competence: Guidelines

Ask quality questions. The more focused and specific you are when asking questions, the more it will be clear to both the customer's conscious and unconscious mind that you have prepared and are meeting with the customer to find a way to help them.

Hazy and rambling questions around the customer's important issues make you appear incompetent. If you notice the customer getting fidgety or distracted, you have some good feedback that your customer would rather be doing other things than talking with you. In other words, you are not being perceived as helping them and, thus, you apparently have no value to them.

(If you want to develop your skills in asking great questions, check out *SPIN Selling* by Rackham, *Solution Selling* by Bosworth, or *Strategic Selling* by Miller and Heiman.)

Learn advanced listening skills. When we discussed compassion, we referenced compassionate listening. To demonstrate competence, there are three other listening skills that need to be applied. These are comprehensive, discerning, and evaluative listening skills.

Comprehensive listeners are good at recognizing key points and links between one point and another, even when the customer's comm-unication is disorganized. You need to listen for how a customer develops her arguments so that you can understand her rationale. You may ask questions to clarify the customer's intention. However, be clear on your questions so if an individual does not understand what you've said, you can re-explain it in terms she does understand.

Discerning listeners want to make sure they have gathered complete information. They do not assume facts that haven't been stated by the customer, even if making that logical leap might be appropriate. You want to know what main issues and end-results the customer desires.

Evaluative listeners are skeptical by nature. When a customer tells them something, they will probe more deeply to understand what is driving the issue inside the customer's business. They listen intently, waiting for the customer to complete his thoughts and presentation before suggesting a plan of action.

Be authentic. Being yourself is critical to being perceived as competent. If your customer sees you as a real, flesh-and-blood human being with your own passions, frailties, and emotions, they are much more likely to begin trusting you more deeply. They will remember you as a whole person.

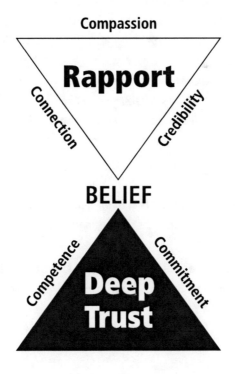

Deep Trust: Commitment

Every sales relationship is in a state of dynamic tension. That tension is often created by three desired-end-results that may be at odds with each other.

1. Your customer wants you to be committed to her.
2. Your company wants you to be committed to maximizing the company's profit.
3. You need to be committed to yourself.

It's tough enough to serve two masters, let alone three.

> *I once consulted with a company whose salespeople needed to persuade three different parties before booking a sale. They of course had to (1) sell to the customer. They also had to (2) sell to their own company's finance office to satisfy that department's demand that customers meet their requirements of financial viability. And, finally, they had to (3) sell to their own company's manufacturing department to ensure that the equipment could be built in a time frame that was reasonable to the company. Two-thirds of the salesperson's time was spent selling to people other than the actual customer.*
>
> *As you might suspect, this company is no longer in business, at least in part because its commitment to protecting itself was out of balance with its commitment to the customer.*

To commit means to entrust, to put into safekeeping, to pledge oneself to a particular course. You can tell when someone is committed to a customer.

The committed person asks, "What can I do to help? How can I do my best to benefit you?" The person who asks, "What is the minimum I can do and still be part of this? What can I get by with?" will not communicate commitment to the customer. The difference shows up in the attitude and is readily observable.

Failure to honor commitments ranks high as a source of customer dissatisfaction. This is because the customer often is relying on the salesperson's word. Like a row of dominoes where each domino stands because the others stand, breaking a commitment sets in motion extensive subsequent ramifications for the customer. It may impact other parts of the customer's business. It may even extend to *their* customers.

The very essence of commitment implies trust. Promising what can't be achieved is a sign that you cannot be trusted.

Co-Creating Commitment

Some salespeople will declare that they want the customer to have a complete say in determining what happens. Yet, salespeople often subtly or overtly override customers' concerns and expressed wishes to do what they, as salespeople, feel is important. If a relationship is to have a chance, people must make their own commitments between themselves about their goals and expectations, as individuals, and as business partners—and they must keep them (or renegotiate if conditions change).

Commitment requires you to explore, develop, and nurture a co-created boundary around the business relationship. You have to work together at it. You each need personal autonomy within that relationship, but you also need to recognize, honor, and respect those agreed-upon and shared boundaries as well.

You can't demand boundaries in advance. You have to negotiate them and promote agreement. You can't impose them on your customer, since you don't have the right to be in charge of the other person. People who try to impose their will on their customer tend to have short-lived business relationships. Customers want to be empowered, not controlled.

Boundaries aren't static. They may need to change over time. This requires both you and the customer to acknowledge and continually review what you expect of each other as the relationship grows. For example, as your customer gains understanding about your product or service, he may need less of your application skill and thus less of your time. This doesn't mean the business relationship is automatically over, unless one of you makes that decision on your own.

What Are You Committed To?

Sales professionals hold dearly to three commitments other than to the customer. The first and most basic of these is a **commitment to a set of values, principles, or beliefs.** These underlying personal principles define the salesperson's uniqueness.

The second is the **commitment to oneself,** to how one acts. To be successful, sales professionals must possess a strong sense of personal integrity and self-confidence. Making a commitment changes the view people have of themselves. Once an active commitment is made, your self-image is squeezed as a result of the pressure to bring your self-image into line with your actions.

Besides serving customers, all organizations target specific results. **Commitment to results** is the third commitment and is largely determined by how clear priorities are, what actions get rewarded, and what risks are being taken to improve intended results.

Effectively demonstrating commitment, whether to customers, to principles, to oneself, or to results is never easy. The truth is, demonstrating commitment is hard work. Wavering commitment is usually seen as no commitment at all. The only way to achieve a reputation for commitment is through determination and persistence. **Genuine commitment stands the test of time and is proven during tough times.**

How someone weathers the storms most clearly demonstrates the depth of their commitment. Epicurus, a philosopher in ancient Greece, stated: "...a captain earns his reputation during the storms." When your competition scores big against you, when the money dries up, or when the glamour of success wears off, that is when it is easiest to compromise your commitments. The real test comes in holding the line against the easy—and tempting—route of compromise.

Fortunately, paying the price that commitment demands has payoffs worth the cost—a reputation for integrity and, even more important, the commitment of others in return. **Commitment is a two-way street. You only get it if you are willing to give it.**

Deep Trust: Consistency

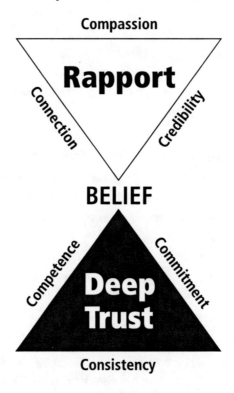

Your customers want you to be consistent. In fact, they rely on it. Prominent psychologists, such as Leon Festinger and Fritz Heider, have uncovered the secrets of consistency. They found that the idea underlying consistency is that we all actively strive to avoid change. That is accomplished, in large part, by being consistent in our beliefs and behaviors.

Any inconsistency acts as an incentive to change either our beliefs or behaviors. When we wake up in the morning, we want to find the roof over our heads, the sun shining, and hot water in the shower. Just as we expect these kinds of physical consistency, we also expect mental and emotional consistency. If we had marriages, families, and jobs yesterday, we expect to find them today in pretty much the same condition.

These physical, mental, and emotional beliefs make up the expectations of how our world operates. This includes the people in it and our relationships with them. The glue that holds all these relationships together is consistency. Consistency helps us to understand the world and our place in it. It allows us to free our minds to focus on other things.

Compromising Consistency

Where are we likely to uncover inconsistency? First, our beliefs and behaviors may be inconsistent with each other. We discover these inconsistencies by looking at situations in which our beliefs would require incompatible behaviors.

Suppose, for example, that I believe that it is wrong to disobey my boss and also believe that it is wrong to tell a lie. Then suppose that one day my boss insists that I tell a customer something that I know to be untrue. I can either obey my boss or I can avoid telling a lie, but I cannot do both. To be consistent, I must modify one or both of these beliefs by examining the reasons I have for accepting them. Then I need to weigh these reasons to see which is more important and worth retaining and which is less important and in need of modification.

Integrity is an often-used word to describe people who behave in ways that are consistent with their beliefs. Polonius, a character in Shakespeare's *Hamlet*, points out how critical such integrity is to life when he says to his son, Laertes:

"This above all: to thine own self be true,
And it must follow, as the night the day,
Thou canst not then be false to any man."

As much as we need consistency, however, there are many occasions when things occur in surprising and unexpected ways—when there is an inconsistency between what we expected and what we got. Someone hands you a luscious-looking tropical fruit. Just looking at it makes you salivate in anticipation of its sweetness. You sniff it and it smells like perfume. You close your eyes, take a big bite and...it's all you can do to keep from spitting out the sour, juicy mass. For a moment everything freezes; time stops as you try to make sense of these two conflicting things—it's supposed to be ambrosia and it tastes like a lemon on steroids.

Dissonance Detracts

The state that arises following this inconsistency is called "dissonance." Dissonance is simply an academic term for the mental, emotional, physiological, and behavioral response that occurs when things do not go the way we expected them to.

One thing that almost immediately happens when we experience dissonance is that we move into mild confusion. We may ask, "What? What was that? I don't get it. Wait a minute." We try to figure out what we missed. Interestingly, we also begin to feel somewhat rattled and upset, almost like we are nervous or anxious. Finally, the physiology of our bodies changes when we experience dissonance. Our heart rate elevates, our blood pressure goes up, and our hands get sweaty.

Dissonance arouses tension and motivates individuals to seek ways of reducing the dissonance. This also explains why hardball persuasion tactics often don't work. When a salesperson explicitly, openly, and directly confronts a customer, the customer is often immediately resistant because of dissonance.

If you, as a salesperson, are inconsistent, you create dissonance with the customer. Inconsistent people may be viewed as confused or indecisive—or at the extreme end, liars.

The congruence of your words and actions is absolutely crucial. Few things destroy customers' trust in salespeople more quickly than saying one thing and doing something different.

People who are dependable and reliable are not only consistent; they also reinforce their commitment to the customer. When you follow through on a promise or pledge to do something, you tell others they can count on you. You can be trusted to "walk your talk." Making a commitment and honoring it builds trust in both your intentions and competence. Your predictable and consistent behavior gives customers a sense of security. They need not spend all their energy figuring out what you are going to do next.

When you don't follow through on a promise, your customer has to make sense of why you didn't perform. He may try to guess what is likely to have happened to you. In a sense, he creates an explanation that resolves the inconsistency (i.e., he's making stuff up).

Once the customer has decided who you are to them, it's too much trouble for them to change their mind. If you're inconsistent with who they've decided you are, you create additional uncomfortable levels of dissonance. The customer then needs to change their beliefs about you or, as it becomes ever more uncomfortable, the level of trust retreats, sometimes to the point that they find it necessary to engage one of your competitors.

Meeting Expectations...

The most difficult kind of consistency to achieve is matching people's expectations. Because you often face a large audience and a wide range of expertise, it's difficult to meet everyone's expectations. You can address this problem by carefully weighing the consistency issues in the context of your target audience and their needs.

...And Matching Your Messages

It is important that there is consistency between your verbal message and your non-verbal message. For example, you're sitting in the customer's office with your arms crossed over your heart while telling him that you're open to hearing what he has to say. This is clearly a mixed message. Your words tell him one thing while your non-verbal cues suggest something very different. This kind of inconsistency may result in customer confusion and withdrawal of business.

To prevent dissonance from happening with your customers, make sure you:

- Know what you've committed to do
- Know what the customer thinks you'll be doing (i.e., what you see and what she sees may be different)
- Pay attention to the details of those commitments
- Keep track of your commitments, no matter how small
- Follow through on every commitment that you are tracking
- Communicate with the customer to ensure that you've met his expectations about the commitment
- Do this consistently

Long-term customers rely on mutually beneficial relationships to accomplish their own agendas.

Wrapping Up Trust

There is a reason we started with a chapter on trust. Without understanding trust, why it's crucial to a long-lasting sales relationship, and how to build trust, first in yourself and then with others, the rest of the material in this book would be far less effective for you. Without this understanding, the best you might hope for is to become a better salesperson.

Knowing and practicing the principles of rapport and deep trust, however, will help you establish a firm foundation upon which you can confidently and effectively stand as you practice the rest of the tools and resources you are about to learn.

Used in the context of trust, they will provide much of what you need to build an outstanding career as a successful sales professional.

2: MOTIVATION

It's mid afternoon and you're calling on a new customer. As you walk into his office you notice several things:

- Along one wall is a floor-to-ceiling bookcase with what seems to be every book written on the individual's profession in the last 50 years.
- On the other three walls are autographed photographs of this person shaking hands with prominent people. You count at least three past presidents of the United States.
- On his credenza behind him are pictures of people whom you interpret to be his family: his wife, two sons, and a daughter.

You realize you have discovered a veritable goldmine of information about the customer that will greatly increase your ability to turn the prospect into a customer.

Now all you have to do is figure out what it means.

What Is Motivation?

Within each person is a blueprint outlining what determines their actions in the world. This blueprint guides their choices about what they feel is important to *be*, to *do*, or to *have*. Psychologists have called these *personal values*. For our purposes, we are going to consider personal values as primary motivators or motivations.

Knowing what a customer's blueprint looks like will impact your chance of achieving success because, if you want to sell successfully, you must assist your customer in getting what they want—in other words, you must understand and serve their primary motivators.

Buying Behavior Begins at Birth

From birth everyone is shaped by their own needs and the demands of society. We adopt these needs and society's goals as our own motivations. These motivations become the foundation for the choices we make throughout the rest of our lives.

Motivations reflect your customer's deepest needs, most compelling interests, and greatest desires. They determine their passions and the reasons behind why they do things in the world—including why they buy. As a sales professional, your challenge is to know your customer's motivations and how they impact their buying behavior.

For example, your customer's motivation for working may be to have a comfortable life, so she chooses a job that she thinks will best help her fulfill that motivation. If your customer is concerned with a comfortable life and you frame your pitch for your product or service in a way that she feels jeopardizes her comfortable life (e.g., "Our PX-3 will revolutionize the way things are done around here"), she will do everything in her power to oppose your suggestion.

You are about to learn the four primary motivators and how to recognize them, so you can communicate to your customer in terms that appeal to and best meet their inner needs.

Where Motivations Come From

When a child is born, their needs are few: air, food, water, clothing and shelter, relief from physical pain, and love. As an adult, they develop special tastes: for food, art/music, lifestyle, and work style. They develop motivations around money, conscience, moral feelings about how people ought to behave. And they gain respect for formal and informal social customs.

As you look at your own life in this context, you will probably see that you sometimes have profound feelings of attraction to or agreement with certain people and practices. You also have distastes, or lists of things that turn you off: laws you might bend, people you don't like, and traditional tokens of culture that you may reject.

Our motivations are products of our culture, conditioned by our biological evolution. Most of a person's values are put in place from birth to about age seven. This process is called *imprinting* and is like copying a book on a copy machine. What is printed on the pages of the original shows up on the copy. During this period, most of our motivations come to us by way of our parents and parent substitutes such as school, church, other children we play with, babysitters, and television.

From about age seven to age thirteen, we go through a process of *modeling*. During this time period, we observe other people who serve as role models whom we imitate, learning something we didn't know before. Perhaps you saw someone hammering a nail and you practiced on the dining room table. (Not all modeling efforts will make parents happy.)

From the age of thirteen to roughly twenty, we go through a period of *socialization*. Basically, we test all of the motivations our parents and others have programmed into us. This is also the period when parents start pulling out their hair as they see all of their good efforts going out the window. If they knew that, after you had finished testing, most of your previously programmed values would remain intact, they might lighten up a little. In fact, one research study says that we keep 95%-98% of all the values that were programmed during the *imprinting* stage.

Much of this conditioning affects how we perceive the world, and as a result influences the actions we take—or don't take. This can have long-lasting effects. (This was illustrated by my day camp water sales story in the preface of this book.)

Motivations & Buying Behavior

There are four primary motivators: **money** (profit), **recognition** (pride), **self-preservation** (peace or protection), and **romantic ideal** (pleasure or fulfillment). We will go into much more detail on these later; however, it will be useful for you to have an awareness of what they are as we proceed.

People will react to benefits that appeal to their primary motivators. However, certain products and activities, by their very nature, may fit one person more closely than they fit another. For example, if you place a high value on having an *exciting life*, you may own a motorcycle, participate in outdoor sports, go on safari, skydive, etc. You might not be the kind of person who has a quiet home in the country, reads fiction in front of the fireplace, or whose only contact with sports is on television.

If a product or service is not presented so that it relates to the buyer's motivations, those products or services might be ignored or devalued. So motivations affect a customer's perception of a problem (or pain), how they search for information, and their beliefs about what is the correct course of action in a particular situation.

Do motivations *directly* affect attitudes, intentions, and buying? No. According to the research available, motivations have only an indirect affect on buying. In most cases, motivations affect buying at an unconscious level. This is great news for you! **When you learn to present your product or service and tie in the key words that accurately reflect the customer's motivations, you can influence their purchase decision at an unconscious level.**

Remember, though, that while this information can be used to manipulate, the key to building a solid foundation of sales success is knowing motivators to support customers in getting what they need.

Appealing to motivators is something advertisers have been doing since the 1960s.

How Advertising Uses Motivations

At the end of World War II, demand for war-related products dropped dramatically. The good news for manufacturers was the five years of pent-up demand for consumer goods that were not being made in order to convert those factories to producing war materiel. People waited months for a new car and often paid a premium (or a bribe) to get bumped higher in line on the waiting list. The manufacturers had it good until about 1948, when demand started to taper off.

The manufacturers went to their advertising agencies and asked, "How come our goods aren't selling?" The advertisers responded, "Because demand has been satisfied." The manufacturers said, "Excuse us, we pay you to <u>create</u> demand." And life was forever changed. Where demand had been created by real need, it now became possible to invent a *perceived* need.

From the advertiser's viewpoint, linking motivations to products is exactly what their job is about. In this way, products become special to the customer. The creative process in advertising uses everything at its disposal, all the tools of persuasion through words and images, to portray the product—and by association, those who consume it—as idealized and deserving of adoration or envy.

When you are on a sales call, sitting face-to-face with your customer, you are the advertising agency, the copywriter, and the graphic artist. The words you use are the tools that create the internal images that will—or will not—move the customer to action.

S.I. Hayakawa—noted psychologist, semanticist, teacher, and writer—likened advertising to poetry and noted that the "copywriter, like the poet, must invest [the product] with significance so that it becomes symbolic of something beyond itself." The task of the copywriter is to poeticize the product or service. Commercials have been described as contemporary myths encouraging us to "perform a substitute act, a symbolic gesture, in which we put coins on the counter and pick up a magic potion or a symbolic object." More specifically, Charles Revson, the founder of the cosmetic company Revlon, once said, "In the factory we manufacture cosmetics; in the store we sell hope."

As a sales professional, your ability to use language to create emotional word pictures is a powerful resource. However, you must be able to correctly classify people by their motivations so that you will know the language and images that are specific to the primary motivations of the customer you are working with.

How Advertisers Classify People

Over the last 50 years, advertisers have developed many different classification systems. These systems started with basic demographics—classifying people by age, gender, income, where they live, etc. Other systems have developed to incorporate psychographics—the motivations and lifestyles of the people in the survey group.

Most of these classifications are fairly complex. The system you will be dealing with here is highly effective, even though it's much simpler.

How You Can Classify People

There are many different motivations as a result of different cultures people are raised in. What motivates people to choose their passions in life, what they would like to be, do, or have, has been the subject of literally thousands of research projects over the last 100 years.

In a late 1950s study, psychologist Frederick Herzberg outlined several major "satisfiers" or motivators in the work environment. The top six were recognition, achievement, the work itself, responsibility, advancement, and salary. In many studies that replicate Herzberg's work, there were four values that kept popping up. They are the ones we mentioned earlier: **money** (profit), **recognition** (pride), **self-preservation** (peace or protection), and **romantic ideal** (pleasure or fulfillment). These four fundamental motivations show up with more frequency than all of the others combined—and these are the ones we work with.

Money (I Want More and More and More)

In the movie *Wall Street,* there is a scene where Gordon Gekko is driving in Manhattan with Bud Fox. Gordon's entire conversation focuses on making and losing money. At one point, he rolls down the limo's window and points out a building that he bought, sold, and made his first big money. Gordon is an example—maybe an extreme example—of a money-motivated person.

An old joke says that money may not be everything, but it's way ahead of whatever is in second place. Since every joke is only funny because there is an element of truth in it, you might think that money would be the prime motivator of most people. You would be wrong. Almost all of the research to date shows that money is often ranked in third or fourth place.

If this seems strange to you, think of money as a catalyst to assist people in getting what they *really* want. When people have enough money, they usually develop a comfort zone around money. More would be nice, but not if they have to work a lot harder to get it. So money diminishes in importance as the person gets *enough*—whatever enough is for them.

Motivation expert Saul Gellerman said it best in *Motivation in the Real World*: "But money is not only inefficient as a motivator: at times it's also close to being unnecessary. There are certain occupations to which eager young recruits are drawn the way flies are drawn to honey. Some examples are publishing, the theater, and jobs in and around filmmaking. The supply of would-be editors, actors, and scriptwriters usually exceeds the demand by a considerable margin. Employers in these industries are able to hold their wage costs way down because their employees not only love their work but are entranced by the lure of getting that 'one big break' that they think is all they need. They may grouse about low pay, but are usually reluctant to take the one step that could put them firmly on the path to better incomes. That would be to enter a profession in which the odds are not so long against them."

The one exception is that **if someone's primary motivator actually is money,** the preceding is not true because they will never get enough. They will always want more.

To find out who is really motivated by money, you need to eliminate people who are merely using money to reach their true motivation. People who fall into this category are those just starting out in their first jobs or who have a lifestyle that is only a notch above poverty. For these people, additional money has not yet yielded diminishing returns. Eventually, these people reach their comfort zones, though, and are unlikely to devote added time or effort to get more money.

Then there are the people who are truly driven by money and the need for ever-greater sums of money. Typically these people are obsessed with money, sometimes to the point of lusting after it. People in this category will sacrifice time, effort, relationships, and business partners to increase their income. They do this even when they already have a great deal of money.

For them, making money is a ritual. They are so focused on making money that they do not last for long in a large corporate atmosphere. Why? Because they quickly figure out that they can't get rich on a paycheck, no matter how good that paycheck is. Their drive for ever-greater sums of money provides all the motivation they need. If you remember Scrooge McDuck, from your childhood comic books, he would be an accurate depiction of being money motivated. You *may* encounter this type of person as a customer.

Money can be gotten in two ways: making it or saving it. **Show these people how your product or service can help them make money or save money and they will pay attention to you and your presentations.**

Recognition (Look at What I've Accomplished)

People who are not in the sales profession often think that sales professionals are motivated by money. Our research indicates that *recognition* is, in fact, their primary motivator.

Donald Trump is an excellent example of someone motivated by recognition. You may think his primary motivation is money, but the money is actually a way for him to gain the recognition he really wants.

Being perceived as affluent is a recognition trait, not a money trait. People motivated by recognition devote a great portion of their incomes to status purchases and leisure pursuits, such as rare wines, stocks, gold jewelry, and country club memberships at rates far above what most others would be comfortable paying. In conversations with these people, you will usually hear about their latest acquisition.

Believing that other people are watching them (whether it's true or not), these people tend to be well groomed, as having a distinctive appearance contributes to their look of success. Some people find that this projected "on-top-of-the-world" air of confidence makes those motivated by recognition unapproachable.

People with a primary value of recognition are very adept politically. They will never say too much—especially to those in authority. They are well skilled in reading other people's hidden motivations.

Goals are critically important to these people, as they want others to know how much they have accomplished in the world. They are motivated toward those goals by a system of immediate rewards from others that acknowledges and affirms their accomplishments. The problem for them is that within a short time after achieving a goal, no matter how significant, their success becomes hollow. Like the song, they will ask, "Is that all there is?" These people can be so driven to accomplish these goals that they can sacrifice personal needs—even their health.

Because they have set it up to seem that their identity lies in what they do, criticism of their performance equals personal rejection. Some people who are obsessed with recognition will attempt to prevent criticism by lying. These people also have an intuitive knowing of how to expand on an idea and make it a success. Taking risks and becoming overextended is not unusual for them. In fact, for them, all things are possible, and they are adept at inspiring others and overcoming resistance to their goals.

The ability to use words is one of their greatest assets. Very often they can be excellent public speakers, willing to research their subject thoroughly and present it with charm and flair.

Many of these people are deeply feeling, though they may occasionally repress these feeling for fear of rejection. They view rejection as an obstacle to being seen.

Their business relationships can be complicated. If they feel hurt or angry, they will withdraw emotionally and work harder, putting people at a greater distance from them.

These people can be motivated by special or unusual recognition.

> *Several years ago, I managed a sales office in which many people were recognition oriented. A good percentage of our business took a long time to bring to fruition, sometimes a year or more.*
>
> *I created a trophy that was awarded only when a salesperson closed a deal that took effort and persistence above and beyond what was thought possible. Although the actual trophy had little monetary worth (a Mack Truck Bulldog mounted on a walnut base), people who had the "Bulldog" trophy were accorded a higher level of status and respect than those who did not.*
>
> *The overall outcome was that our region closed more deals than any other region within the same company. This was a direct result of people trying to be the next trophy winner (i.e., striving to gain recognition).*

If you, as a sales professional, are recognition oriented and your client is as well, here's a word of caution: It's important that your client be put in the spotlight and you take a back seat. Too often, salespeople are so good at self-promotion that they inadvertently cause the sales call to end without a satisfactory conclusion by shifting the spotlight to themselves. Sales professionals will recognize that the job with a recognition-motivated customer is to shine the spotlight on the customer.

Self-Preservation (Don't Rock the Boat!)

Do you remember Linus from the "Peanuts" cartoon series? He carries with him a security blanket. In early cartoons, he would break into a nervous sweat when his blanket was taken from him.

His behavior reflected an attitude of, "Who am I without it?" Self–preservation people have their own sort of blanket. They are all fundamentally attached to something or someone that they really, really need, that defines, to a significant extent, who they are. It may be their job, their career, their title, or something else that fulfills this for them.

At work, the self-preservation value is all about making sure that the economic lifeline is firmly fastened to a steady source of cash. They perceive the company they work for as powerful enough, and committed enough, to protect them against whatever they fear most (e.g., losing their job, losing income, losing their security). For this person, one of their worst fears is of not knowing where their next check is going to come from. **Do keep in mind that it is not the *money* that motivates them; it is the *security*.**

The key in selling them is to show how you will help them maintain the status quo and strengthen their position of security. In other words, they will view financial increase—even if it's literally money in their pocket—as a temporary benefit and it will not motivate them to action.

Self-preservation people are factually oriented individuals who may repress their ability to make decisions so that they can maintain a harmonious relationship between themselves and others. However, they are also social people who continually seek to connect with a stable group that has well-defined values. They feel this need because they experience a pervading sense of insecurity.

As a way of compensating for their lack of self-confidence and inner authority, they depend on the stability and values of the group. This is one reason they might feel so threatened and be hesitant to confront their work group directly. If your product or service is perceived in any way to threaten this stability, they will fiercely resist buying.

Taken to an extreme, this motivation becomes dysfunctional and leads to striving to feel safe and secure by following the rules. Their basic life issue is risking, and their prime psychological addiction is fear, especially of not fitting in, of doing things wrong, and of displeasing those who are important to them. Even when there is evidence that things are not working under the established rules, they often stick their head in the sand and insist on preserving the status quo.

If they must stick their neck out, they will take only very calculated risks. If they determine that the chances are good they will be able to accomplish what they have planned to do, they will proceed. When a new idea is proposed, they might comment either that it has never been done this way before or ask, "Why fix what isn't broken?" Threaten their value and they will have trouble focusing on what they need to do next.

Self-preservation people want the protection that authority affords, yet they may become upset at feeling confined by demands and expectations of them when they are in authority. They also can resent the fact that when they are in authority they feel vulnerable to criticism for making choices that don't work out.

Although they respect and value other people's judgment, just because they may elicit the ideas of others is no guarantee that these ideas will factor into their final solution or that the final decision will be made in a democratic fashion. And when people in the group disagree, the alternative approach for self-preservation people may be to spend time using dialogue to bring dissenters around to their way of thinking. **In general, self-**

preservation people prefer to have consensus, because that
provides them with the security and protection of group
responsibility.

The need for them to feel both closely connected to the group and
to maintain harmony creates wariness that makes trust difficult
for them. However, they trust completely the few who prove
themselves to be loyal. Social charm masks their underlying
caution until they feel confident that they can correctly read other
people's reactions. Their desire for acceptance and their fear of
rejection combine continually to keep them off balance.

These people are extremely loyal to their "family," whether it be a
traditional nuclear family, a community or an intimate social
group, or an organization or business. In the family they are
faithful teachers who both communicate and model high
standards and moral values. Their commitment to family and their
need to belong often unite to make them the guardians of family
tradition and history.

These people love "inside information" about everyone they are
connected with and can become irritated if important information
is withheld from them. Knowing all the facts, real or suspected,
makes them feel they have earned the status of trusted confidant.
Being kept in the dark fills them with self-doubt, causing them to
feel insecure about their acceptance in the group.

While it might be easy to view customers motivated by self-
preservation as pushovers, be careful not to do anything that
upsets the delicate balance of their world. If these people feel that
any of your actions put them at risk, you will see the fire-
breathing dragon side of their nature.

When you do business with them, they are likely to create a "psychological contract" as well as have a business contract. While this psychological contract may not be a formal agreement, every statement you make about what you are going to do adds more detail to it. While not written on paper, nor enforceable in a court of law, in their mind they believe it to be real. **It will serve you to be aware of each commitment you make to them, and to make sure you fulfill it or re-negotiate it with them, or you will find it difficult to close a sale with them.**

Sometimes security masquerades as dependency. Consequently, to gain a sense of security, these people will play on your sympathy and want to be seen by you as a "nice guy" in order to enhance the likelihood of your making sure their orders are given top priority. This is especially true if you have a product or service that is scarce and in high demand. These customers do not want to do anything that will interrupt their nice, safe, regular supply.

Self-preservation people are more likely to be conformists, adopting the corporate uniform, resembling others in action and expressed beliefs. The underlying aim of these people is to seek safety in acceptance, hoping that the crowd will protect them from misfortune.

Because these people take only calculated risks, before they purchase any goods or services they determine that the chances are good they will be able to assimilate those products or services into their environment, without disrupting it. **Lacking confidence in their own ability to decide, they prefer to trust what is known and repeat what they have done before.**

So if you have identified this person as capable of signing the purchase order, do not be surprised if they delay and get feedback from others in their sphere of influence. As they prefer consensus, they will search out the opinions of others, using a dialogue style of decision-making. You can make these people feel safe by acknowledging this process and even suggesting it take place.

Whether decisions are made by the group or independently, these people carry them out slowly, carefully, and responsibly. This approach allows time to inform, explain, and discuss difficulties that may arise.

Romantic Ideal (Making Life Wonderful)

In the movie *Don Juan DeMarco*, Johnny Depp plays a modern-day version of Don Juan and his time in a mental institution. While the movie is lighthearted and not very deep, it portrays a true romantic ideal and the way a patient's fantasies affect his doctor's reality. The movie cleverly illustrates how a romantic-ideal person can cloud the division between what's real and what isn't.

The basic life issue for the romantic idealist is to feel good or happy. These are feeling-oriented people who focus their thinking and calculating on making their lives easier. Their minds and bodies are in perpetual motion. Romantic idealists are always searching for the perfect sunset.

These highly intuitive people are often ahead of their time. **When dealing with these customers, focus your discussion on how your product or service can make life easier for the company and, more importantly, for them.**

The outside world can be a place in which discomfort and pain are experienced, so these people prefer to live inside their head. In this way they protect themselves from becoming entangled in the stress of daily life. Instead, they make plans to salve, solve, and save. In other words, they indulge in what other people would call fantasy. These fantasies protect them from having to live within the confines of painful reality.

One sales challenge you face with these people is that they are compulsive optimists, not realists. If they perceive a problem, they will always think there is a solution. This is good news for you, especially if you are offering *pain relief.* Not being realists, however, they may not take the action steps necessary to implement the solution. You will need to lay out these action steps for them and encourage them to completion. Otherwise, they will stay happily locked into their fantasy "perfect plan" that never actually gets executed.

Though shrinking from pain, they thrive on positive challenges. Challenge them and their mind is filled with visions of how to exceed any expectations contained in the challenge. Just as quickly, however, the next challenge appears—how to get others to enact their plans. The thought of the hard work needed to accomplish their newly devised solution sends them retreating into the solitude of their fantasy world.

Their craving for pleasure is frequently expressed in the challenge of learning new things. They are usually attracted to the latest ideas, though they often find themselves unable to apply their newfound knowledge in practical ways.

When they must present plans to their co-workers, they can be as subtle as a jackhammer. Rejection only causes them to refine the plan and figure out new ways to present it. To them, details and implementation are the responsibility of others.

The romantic idealist is always looking for ways to improve the organization, in the sometimes-false belief that change equals growth. These people frequently advocate constant change, which puts them in direct conflict with self-preservationists. What's more, they only present the vision; they expect others to accomplish the changes presented.

These people like to talk things out. So discussing all the pros and cons of proceeding with your offering is recommended. Make the discussions animated and impersonal, leading to negotiation and some compromise. If there are others in the customer's organization who also support your conclusion, so much the better.

If this process becomes personal or painful to anyone, watch out! Romantic-ideal people will summarily shut down the sales process and, if in authority, will cancel all further discussions. It's your job to make sure that all loose ends are tied up, yet done in a way that does not pin these people down. If you can show them how their decision preserves flexibility, you are ahead of the game.

These people value relationships above all else. If you build an appropriate level of trust, they will go around almost any obstacle to do business with you. Family and friends are very important to these people.

Obviously, leisure activities especially interest this crowd. These people do not avoid pleasure nor hide from amusement. The fun-enjoyment-excitement people seem to be ones who want to "stop and smell the roses," appreciating whatever life is giving them at that moment. In spite of an often bleak present, these people enjoy what they have and feel optimistic and confident about the future. This group probably spends more money on recreational equipment, sporty cars, and vacations than the rest of the population.

Motivation Hierarchy

It's fair to say that most people have all four motivations somewhere in their internal programming. What is important is how a person ranks them. This is an unconscious process.

People will sacrifice less vital motivations to ensure that the most important motivations are kept intact. How the prospect ranks their values will influence your approach in adapting to them.

If the customer ranks money over recognition, your discussion or presentation needs to communicate first how your product or service will help bring in more money and, second, how the prospect will be recognized for that effort. When you know the hierarchy, you will begin to tap into the prospect's unconscious negotiation strategy.

Identifying Individuals' Motivations

Archaeologists dig up ancient civilizations. From various pottery fragments and other artifacts they can determine, with remarkable accuracy, how people in that civilization lived their lives. You can do the same thing by understanding the artifacts in your customer's office.

You have seen a customer's office and the artifacts in his work environment. You have identified a couple of motivator clues. How do you determine which motivator is at the top of his hierarchy? If you know, you can structure your presentation in a way that motivates him from a totally unconscious level and increase the likelihood of accomplishing your sales goals because you increase the likelihood of meeting his needs.

Here are two specific ways of determining the ranking a customer places on his motivations:

1. *Observe*. Study the customer, his surroundings, evidence of hobbies and products he now uses and, most importantly, the symbols he has around him or in the office and their placement.
2. *Listen*. Each motivation has a specific language. Most people will unconsciously use the language that represents their dominant motivation(s).

Observing Symbols

If you've ever taken basic psychology class, you may remember that we have symbols around us that impart special meaning. Often they are a representation of an experience we've had. For example, what kind of car do you drive? Is it an SUV or a fast sports car? Cars are often much more than transportation; they reflect who we think we are.

> *One of my favorite sales calls was with an executive vice president who loved BMWs. In fact, he owned two. At that time, I was on my third BMW. We talked about driving and owning BMWs for about 25 minutes. With about 10 minutes remaining before he needed to go into another meeting, he asked me to summarize what I would be doing for his salespeople. When I was finished, he looked at me and said, "Sounds great, when can we begin?" That was the entire sales call.*

He and I are both recognition oriented, and tapping into
his need for recognition and using the "connection" part of
the trust model was all the close needed.

Symbols reflect our feelings and experiences. A symbol allows us
to recall special events in our lives, recreating that moment in
vivid detail. We might even re-experience the surge of emotions
when that symbol is present. All of these feelings, sounds, and
images, even smells and tastes, are tied to simple symbols.

How close or far away the symbol is from where the customer sits
also has meaning. This is the language of *proxemics,* the study of
spatial distances between individuals and symbols in different
cultures and situations.

Some architects take proxemics very seriously. They know that by
organizing space differently, they can influence people to behave
differently, even though the situation may be the same.

For example, take two physicians' waiting rooms. Strangers don't
usually talk to each other prior to a doctor's appointment. By
changing the furniture arrangement of one of the rooms to
promote interaction (e.g., chairs facing each other or in close
proximity), strangers will be more open to beginning
conversations with one another.

Take all of this into consideration as you scan your customer's
office. For example, are pictures of the family on the desk facing
the customer, behind her on the credenza, or off to the side?
Pictures in front, facing the customer, indicate that the family is of
primary importance to the person, behind them often means that
the family is viewed as a support mechanism, and off to the side
they are an auxiliary part of the individual's life.

Money-motivated people will often have items on their desk that represent either making money or saving money. Certain business magazines that are geared toward money, such as *Red Herring,* may be an example. High-quality (read expensive) pen and writing pad sets are another example.

Recognition-motivated people might have awards, pictures of themselves with important people, trophies, etc. The closer these objects are to their seat, the more important they are, and the more willing they will be to talk to you about the experience.

Self-preservation people will have an office that follows standard corporate decoration. Pictures on the wall may even have been placed there by the corporation. Sometimes you'll notice stacks of paper around the perimeter of their desk, almost looking like a fortress wall. One banker I know of had stacks of paper on all surfaces of his office, including his desk, credenza, conference table, tops of filing cabinets, seats around the conference table, and around the perimeter of his office walls. He had so much paper that he had moved to the vacant office next door. The implicit communication was, "Look how much I'm involved in; you can't possibly fire me."

Romantic-ideal people will often have posters of exotic or tropical places on their walls, or perhaps even a bowl with wine corks. One romantic idealist I called on had a map of the world behind his desk with pin flags in various places and one group of pin flags connected with thread. When I asked him about the map he said, "Those are all the places I've traveled in the world." When I asked about the ones connected with thread he told me, "That was the trip I took around the world when I graduated from high school." Not too unusual, except that this gentleman was in his 60s and his trip around the world had probably taken place more than 40 years previously.

Each symbol that a person has put in their office has significant psychological meaning to them. If you were to study Freudian or Jungian dream psychology, you would gain an understanding of the internal motivations that person has.

So, consider the story at the start of this chapter. What did all the clues mean?

It's mid afternoon and you're calling on a new customer. As you walk into the individual's office you notice several things:

- *Along one wall is a floor-to-ceiling bookcase with what seems to be every book written on the individual's profession for the last 50 years.*

  From that we now know that the person wants us to recognize how much he knows.

- *On the other three walls are autographed photographs of this person shaking hands with prominent people. You count at least three past presidents of the United States.*

  From the sheer volume of the photos and the prominence of the people in them, it's apparent that this person is highly motivated by recognition.

- *On his credenza behind him are pictures of people that you interpret to be his family: his wife, two sons, and a daughter.*

  The placement of this photo is the most telling clue, indicating that he relies on his family as a support system. They "back him up."

Though you started the call with little to go on as to how to present to this individual, you now have a solid foundation of evidence to give you confidence in being able to communicate to him in a way he will both understand and respond favorably to.

Listening to the Words

As a salesperson, you know that you need to listen to your customers, if only to understand clearly what they need. As a sales professional, you are aware that if you listen carefully, you'll actually begin to hear them use words that represent their motivations. This isn't an accident; words have specific meaning to the individual using them.

The following are fairly complete word lists. After you've spent some time listening to your customers, you'll begin to notice that there is a pattern of words they use. Knowing what's underneath the words allows you to accurately understand your customers' motivations.

Money Words

Money is wired two different ways: saving money and making money. People interested in *saving money* would be motivated by these key words:

a good value	at cost	bargain
budget	cut-rate	discounted
economical	inexpensive	nest-egg
pecuniary	penny-pinching	thrifty
undervalued		

People interested in *making money* would be motivated by these key words:

appreciation	assets	bonanza
bonds	boon	booty
bread	bucks	cash
commissions	commodious	costly
deeds	dinero	dividends
dough	earnings	enriched
equity	exorbitant	expensive
extravagant	fatten	financial
fiscal	formula	fortune
fruitful	generous	godsend
golden opportunity	grow	growth potential
heap	high yields	highly regarded
increase	inflate	inheritance
interest	investment	limitless
lion's share	loads	loot
lucre	luxurious	magnify
markets	megabucks	mint
miracle	monetary	money-making
moolah	multitude	notes
payoff	pocketbook	posh
possessions	priceless	profitable
profits	promotable	prosper
rich	riches	royalty
salary	scads	solid gold
spoils	stake	stocks
success	top dollar	treasure
treasured	trove	trust
valuable	wealth	windfall

Recognition Words

People interested in recognition would tend to use these words:

a towering achievement	a Who's Who of	acclaimed
accomplished	ace	achievement
apex	appreciation	attention
awe-inspiring	awesome	birthright
blockbuster	cachet	celebrated
class	commanding	consideration
crème de la crème	distinction	dominant
echelon	elegant	elite
estate	esteemed	exclusive
fame	famed	famous
gifted	glorious	good standing
has won the respect of	heritage	honored
illustrious	influential	landmark
legendary	majestic	major
mark	masterly	matchless
notable	note	noteworthy
notice	of high repute	office
outstanding	peerless	perception
perfect	position	post
preeminent	prestige	prestigious
privileged	prominent	rank
recognized	recommended	regard
renowned	reputation	revered
seasoned	selective	seniority
significant	stance	station
stature	status	stunning
superb	superlative	superstar
surpasses	the absolute	the most imitated
the most talked about	the Rolls Royce of	top-notch
tops	triumphant	uncommon

| unparalleled | veteran | VIP treatment |
| world-class | world-famous | |

Self-Preservation Words

People interested in self-preservation would tend to use these words:

bulwark against	carefulness	caution
comfy	confident	count on
defends you	dependable	durable
forget about	full protection	guards you
haven	hazard free	heavy-duty
heavyweight	indestructible	insulates you
lasts	no more guesswork	peace of mind
possessing dignity	potential injury	protects
puts your mind at ease	reinforced	rely on
rigorous	rugged	safe
saves you	secluded	secure
security	shelters you	sleep secure
snug	soothing	sound
stability	stands up to	strong
tamper-proof	total privacy	total security
tough	trusted	unswerving
vulnerable	will last	you can depend on
your assurance of	you're in control	

Romantic Ideal Words

People interested in fulfilling their romantic ideal would tend to use these words:

adventure	adventurous	allure
aura	beautiful	beckons
beguiling	bewitching	boldness
bravery	breathless	burning
burnished	captivating	charming
coarse	cool	corrupt
courage	creamy	crystalline
daring	dazzling	delightful
dreamlike	earthiness	earthy
effervescent	enchanting	enthralling
evocative	excitement	exquisite
glowing	gorgeous	handsome
haunting	holding hands	incandescent
intimate	irresistible	kindled
kissing	lovely	luminous
magic	magical	memorable
miracles	moist	mood
moonlit	moving	mystery
mystical	mythic	passionate
picturesque	pleasing	radiant
rainbow-colored	rapturous	ravishing
ripe	romance	rowdy
satisfying	savage	smoldering
spell	storybook world	sun-swept
sunlit	superstition	tantalizing
tempting	thrill	timeless realm
titillating	torrid	tropical
uncontrolled	unreliable	untamed
vivid	voluptuous	voracious

| whisper-soft | windswept | winsome |
| witchcraft | wizardry | wondrous journey |

As you develop skill at listening, people will literally tell you their motivations.

Mastery: Adapting to Your Client

Adapting to others means working with your customer by respecting her motivations while understanding and respecting your own needs at the same time. If you feel like you need to "change" your customer to persuade her to buy your product or service, you're setting yourself up for buyer's remorse. **If *you* become the source of motivation to own the product or service, then that motivation leaves just as soon as *you* walk out the door.**

A more elegant approach is to understand the customer's motivations and present your product or service in a way that ties into it.

In some selling situations, this can be difficult because you may call on people who have completely different motivations from yourself. Sometimes you call on people whose motivations are so diametrically opposed to yours that you have to question whether you even want to do business with them. For the sake of this discussion, let's assume that you are calling on people you want to do business with. Therefore, it's in your best interests to learn how to adapt.

Once you've identified the primary motivations of your customer, you can begin to modify your benefit statements by using the specific words supplied in this chapter. For example, your product or service might have benefit 1 and benefit 2—let's say it eats fewer oats and produces less waste. Your own experience tells you that these two benefits are the primary reason most people buy your product or service.

Most often we will tell our customer about the benefit using words that fit our own motivation. For example, if I'm recognition motivated, I might say something like, "The Seabiscuit model consumes fewer oats and releases less waste, giving you the opportunity to gain a commanding market share." The word "commanding" works well with people who are recognition oriented.

However, this statement probably won't work that well with people who are money, self-preservation, or romantic-ideal motivated. You would need to change the language and insert language that is consistent with their motivation. For example:

Money: "The Seabiscuit model consumes fewer oats and releases less waste, giving you the opportunity to gain a more profitable market share."

Self-Preservation: "The Seabiscuit model consumes fewer oats and releases less waste, giving you an assurance of dependability."

Romantic Ideal: "The Seabiscuit model consumes fewer oats and releases less waste, giving you the opportunity to dazzle your market."

There are two common mistakes salespeople make when using this skill:

1. They often put too many motivation words into the same sentence. So, keep in mind that, like soup, lightly salting your communication with specific words brings the flavor

out. Too much salt will cause your customer to cringe and possibly reject your efforts. For example: "The Seabiscuit model consumes fewer oats and releases less waste, giving you a spectacular opportunity to triumph by gaining a commanding market share while being recognized as a world-class market leader." This is great for soap operas, but not so great for sales professionals.

2. Salespeople often present these so that it is their own company that has the money, recognition, self-preservation, romantic ideal. Using our same example: "The *world-class* OldGrayMare company will provide you with a product that consumes fewer oats and releases less waste." The customer wants to know how he will be recognized within his own company or amongst his peers. Unless he is concerned with buying a product made by a world-class company, the statement above may actually have a negative impact.

The Bottom Line on Motivation

Customers buy based on the internal and unconscious factors that motivate them to action. Salespeople often get caught up in selling their "expertise," instead of connecting with and understanding the motivations of the person sitting across from them. They prominently promote themselves and list a string of accomplishments or affiliations in the biographies that dominate their brochures. They "sell" functional results.

Once you realize that customers "buy" a desired-end-result that ties into their motivations, you have an incredible power to address your sales pitch to satisfy what the customer believes she needs.

On the whole, most customers don't know the difference between average and excellent results. They don't know what is a reasonable cost for quality. They can't judge the technical competence of you or another salesperson. To distinguish ourselves as sales professionals, we need to ensure excellence in everything with which our customers come in contact and to create value by linking in to their motivations.

Knowing the four motivators, understanding how to recognize the customer's prime motivator(s)—and how to keep them separate from your own—and becoming skilled in communicating the benefits of the product or service you offer in terms of your customer's motivators will amplify your effectiveness and enhance your sales success record.

3: BEHAVIOR

Jack has been selling for about five years. He's taken a number of sales training courses, knows his products well, and is comfortable calling on his clients. Recently, there was a change at one of his customers. A new person has taken the place of the buyer he used to call on—a person with whom he had had a very comfortable and friendly relationship.

Thinking it should be an easy transition, Jack meets the new buyer for the first time. He starts off by telling stories about the old buyer and how they had a great time playing golf together, etc. The new buyer interrupts him and starts asking detailed questions about one of the products that Jack had previously sold the company. Jack doesn't have the answer to some of the questions and tells the buyer that he would need to talk with engineering first.

The buyer, who seemed cold throughout the meeting, tells Jack, "Well, next time you come, why don't you bring one of your engineers with you. That way I'm sure to accurately get the answers I need." With that comment, he then excuses Jack, saying that he needs to meet with two other vendors.

In the last chapter, you discovered a lot about people's motivations—what they want to be, do, or have—and how you can use this knowledge to more effectively assist them in achieving those things with your product or service. However, there is another aspect of this you need to know: how they *go about* getting the things they want. To understand this, you need the key to understanding people's behaviors.

Different Strokes for Different Folks

Not surprisingly, different people have different behaviors. Your success in sales is directly related to your ability to *adapt* to another person's behavioral approach to life. The simple fact is, the sales professional with the most behavioral flexibility will close more sales.

We all have our own styles of behavior. However, **natural behavior on your part that is perceived by the customer as inappropriate (according to their personal behavior style) could result in your being shown the door very early in the sales call**. So, how do you distinguish appropriate from inappropriate behavior? How do you know when behavior that is natural for you is an inappropriate response to the prospect or customer?

You actually can know these things, and the method is surprisingly simple. Not necessarily easy, but simple once you practice it.

Let's suppose you've just had an excellent day of meetings with a number of potential customers. Each person represents a substantial amount of new business and income to you. Going over your notes from each meeting, you summarize how each person behaved.

Prospect One: Doreen is abrupt and to the point. What I first noticed about her was a firm handshake and an interest in getting down to business immediately. She kept asking "bottom-line" questions. She had a tendency to cut me off when I was discussing some of the fine points about doing business with our company. At the end of the meeting, I noticed that she seemed to be checked out, like her mind was elsewhere.

Prospect Two: Irving was friendly and very sociable. When other people stuck their head into Irving's office, he took the time to answer their questions. He didn't seem to mind the interruptions. As I got into the details of our company's offering, he seemed to lose interest in the conversation. At the end of the meeting, I closed with a compliment on his pictures on the wall and he became animated again and told me about the artist being a personal friend of his.

Prospect Three: Stephen was fairly low-key and easygoing. At first he seemed to be nervous when I talked about the changes going on in the market and how it might be impacting his company. We discussed his needs and often he would pause and consider what I was saying, acting as if he was in deep thought.

Prospect Four: When I first met Christy, she seemed somewhat "distant." While her office was meticulous, what I noticed most was her detailed and carefully prepared questions. I thought she was ready to move forward and when I asked her about placing an order she told me, "I can't move that fast; there are many other details I need to consider before placing an order with you."

How would you adapt to each of the four potential customers? Which one would be the easiest to sell and which one would be the most difficult? The information below will help you answer these questions.

What Is Behavior?

Understanding behavior is not new. As far back as ancient Greece, Hippocrates, the father of modern medicine, addressed this, saying that there were four behavioral approaches to life:

- choleric (hot-tempered)
- sanguine (naturally cheerful)
- melancholic (gloomy thoughts and fears)
- phlegmatic (sluggish or apathetic)

In modern times (the last 100 years), two approaches have become dominant for behavior classification in the corporate world. The first looks at 16 different factors. It has been called various names, the most recognized of which is the MBTI or Myers-Briggs Type Indicator. It can be very complex and it takes time and a fair amount of training to reach a conclusion with it.

The second is the DISC style, built largely on the work of Dr. William Marston. We use the DISC style because it is a much simpler approach to understanding a customer's view of their world. It is easier to accurately determine the major components of a person's style using this approach, and you can arrive at very useful information quite quickly once you get familiar with it.

The DISC approach focuses on understanding behavior based on two factors. The first has to do with how *outgoing* or *reserved* the individual is. People who are **outgoing** tend to:
- Be risk takers
- Be more dramatic in body language
- Openly and readily express opinions
- Make initial contact (eye contact or handshake)
- Bend or break company policies

People who are *reserved* tend to:
- Avoid risks
- Be non-dramatic in presenting information
- Keep their opinions to themselves
- Let the other party make the first move
- Rigidly adhere to company policies and rules

The second factor has to do with an individual's approach to business. People are either *task focused or people focused.* *Task-focused* people will tend to:
- Talk about the work at hand
- Be somewhat cool and aloof
- Have definite expectations about what other people do
- Be more cautious

People-focused individuals will tend to:
- Talk about the people they work with
- Be more open and warm in their discussions
- Be flexible about expectations toward others
- Be more enthusiastic

Taking these two theories together you come up with four basic variations in behavioral style, which we'll describe as:
- D—demanding, directing, or domineering (**outgoing** and **task** focused)
- I—interacting, inspiring, or influencing (**outgoing** and **people** focused)
- S—supporting, stabilizing, or steadying (**reserved** and **people** focused)
- C—conscientious, cautious, or correcting (**reserved** and **work** focused).

Understanding behavioral styles would be easy if a person were just one style or another. Life isn't quite that simple, though, and almost every individual demonstrates a mix of the four types of behavior. You rarely find a person who only expresses one style and none of the other three. After profiling more than 11,000 sales professionals, I find that the vast majority have one preferred style and a second that rounds it out. The other two styles will be less expressed.

So you might have a prospect whose primary expression is "I" and secondary expression is "C." For this person, "D" and "S" would be relatively unexpressed.

What is true for your customers is also true for you. Different salespeople will have different approaches based on their own behavioral style. Research suggests that salespeople who know their own style can more easily adapt to their customer's style.

Each style has its own positives and negatives. There is no one best selling style—and there's certainly no "right" or "wrong" style. **In general, your success in sales is a function of your ability to adapt your style based on the needs of the sales situation.**

TYPES OF BEHAVIOR

"D" Behavior – Demanding, Directing, Domineering

Doreen is a doer. She looks for new challenges and opportunities. She has lofty goals and is always reaching for and focusing on success. She lets you know where you stand. Her co-workers call her dominant, iron-willed, determined, and decisive. Failure does not discourage her—she keeps trying new things until she finds what works.

Doreen is not really interested in "how" things get done or the details required to complete a project. Being somewhat compulsive, she stirs the pot and makes changes when she thinks they are needed. If she is in charge, she tells people, "Do it my way." Doreen makes up her mind quickly and moves on to the next agenda item.

While having many of the answers, Doreen may not be popular with her co-workers. Other people often feel insecure around her because she focuses on what needs to get done, not the person or relationship. Her best work is done when no one else is around. When the project is large, she breaks it up into workable chunks and delegates the menial tasks to others, though she continues to wield control.

Doreen is open to new or non-conventional ideas. She often bypasses peer constraints of her work group to listen to imaginative or innovative solutions. This sometimes gets her into trouble, because she has a hard time acknowledging her own shortcomings that may prevent the idea from being implemented. For example, if the new idea turns out to not contribute to one of her goals, she quickly loses interest in it. Or if she senses that control of the idea is being placed elsewhere, she either fights for control or removes herself from the project.

Wanting to be in control, Doreen is capable of careful planning and strategic manipulation of people and situations to ensure her goals are met. She is always looking for ways to reshape or overcome obstacles to her goals.

In situations where her individualism is limited, she may become aggressive and combative. This same behavior occasionally shows itself when she doesn't get her way. While she normally prefers to give the details of an activity to someone else to do, under pressure her need for control and high expectations for performance cause her to complete the activity alone or to interfere with the efforts of others to whom she has delegated the details.

"I" Behavior – Interacting, Inspiring, Influencing

Irving is entertaining, emotionally expressive, and sociable. His spontaneity helps him create a work environment that is informal and casual. Being a gregarious person, he makes friends easily and quickly. Your status, looks, style, and background are not important to Irving, as he is an accepting person. Because of his accepting nature, Irving has an extensive network of contacts both within and outside of his company. Relationships are of primary importance to him.

Having an innate sense of curiosity, Irving wants to "know everything." He constantly asks lots of questions. His mind is quick and he jumps from topic to topic, like a radio being tuned in to and out of different stations. This "knowing everything" is really just surface knowledge that he uses to provide "fun facts" to lubricate interactions with others. He doesn't really know all the details of some of the things he talks about, though he would like you to think he does.

Irving seeks approval and strives to be the center of attention with other people. He doesn't spend much time being alone and will stop for a chat or invite others into his office or workplace. Irving is unlikely to miss any social activities connected with his work. Regardless of the activity, he tends to take advantage of the opportunity to be with people. He enjoys serving on or heading up committees, meetings, and conferences.

Irving is good at promoting and creating enthusiasm for his own ideas. Pulling from his vast network of friends, he makes referrals and personally promotes the credibility of his colleagues and his organization. He is well skilled as a "door opener" for new salespeople.

Because he is naturally optimistic, Irving may not think in enough depth about the situation or problems he is facing. He relies on your ability to see solutions and trusts that you will come up with the correct solutions for the problems. If you cannot express yourself well, he may have difficulty working with you.

Irving is more interested in the relationships he builds than the work he needs to complete. He has difficulty with time management. In the extreme, he is late for meetings and fails to meet deadlines. Under pressure, he becomes less organized or less aware of his time constraints.

Irving likes new ideas and solicits the suggestions of others. Often he will base his decisions on feelings rather than on facts. Even though he is curious, he falls short of gathering all the facts, instead resorting to "trial and error" or "shotgun" approaches— perhaps trying every possible solution that comes to mind until he finds one that works. When it comes time to implement, he has other things to do and delegates the details to someone else. So, if Irving makes a commitment to get back to you with some important details, he might not follow through.

Because Irving has an abundance of energy and enthusiasm, he attracts and inspires others. Harry Truman once said that leadership is the ability to inspire others to work and make them enjoy doing it. This statement sums up Irving and shows his subtle style of leadership. Irving thinks up the ideas and charms others into carrying them out to a productive conclusion.

"S" Behavior – Supporting, Stabilizing, Steadying

Stephen is low-key and easygoing, taking a moderate stand on issues. He prefers to think things through before acting. He gets results by cooperating with others and his co-workers consider him to be patient, helpful, and obliging. At work and at home he has a small circle of friends.

Stephen is most comfortable with a steady, predictable environment. He has regular work habits and well-developed plans for obtaining results. His ability to perform routine tasks for an extended period of time makes him a popular choice for inclusion on major projects.

Stephen creates lists, charts, and graphs to help keep him organized. He is a natural at time management and anything that creates or preserves "order." In fact, his office may be perfectly organized with drawers marked, binders correctly labeled, and few if any unneeded items laying around. He comments, "When your work is organized, you can put your hands on anything you need instantly."

Stephen is a good listener. Seeking to accommodate the wishes of his co-workers, his easy style helps create compromise in conflict situations. He promotes harmony in any situation he is involved with and is tolerant of others' shortcomings.

Stephen's communication style is indirect. He is reluctant to talk about his accomplishments, viewing it as bragging. As a result, his skills and talents may not be fully utilized or appreciated by others. For example, if he offers an idea, he does so in the form of a suggestion. He prefers to make decisions in a slower, more measured way that can insure predictable results.

When starting a new project, Stephen may need some help. He is less likely to initiate a new activity on his own. Being somewhat of a perfectionist, he sometimes has difficulty in completing projects, putting aside work that is essentially complete for later "refinement." Stephen's style prevents him from developing quick and dirty ways to accomplish tasks; he is always thorough.

Being an asset on committees, he asks lots of questions about the work the committee is to accomplish. He will ask questions that are often overlooked by other members. For example, if the company is looking to relocate, he will be the person who asks, "What's the cost to rent the building? How many people do you think will be willing to drive the extra five miles? How much are we going to pay per square foot? Is there a demand for this activity? Do you realize that the move-in dates you've chosen are on Easter weekend?" Without Stephen's balance, many committees would go wild with enthusiasm without fully considering the repercussions.

Stephen may have some fear of disorganization and instability. These fears can make it challenging for him to create or foster change within his organization. If the needed change happens abruptly, Stephen will multiply his efforts to reinstate the status quo. He could end up somewhat demoralized. A guiding hand that takes him step-by-step through the change, helping him see that the outcome matches his desired-end-result will make the changes much more palatable for Stephen. He will regroup his inner and outer resources, and develop a new "status quo."

"C" Behavior – Conscientious, Cautious, Correcting

Christy is meticulous, calculating, and precise in the work she does. Being logical and analytical, she examines each situation she encounters and bases her decisions on the facts. She is able to combine information from very different sources and integrate it into an action plan after completing her analysis. She is concerned about expectations of others and needs well-defined standards of performance.

Engaging in extensive careful preparation before undertaking any project, Christy does everything within her ability to ensure success. She will work to master new skills privately before demonstrating them publicly. Her continual focus on personal and professional quality makes her demanding of the same from co-workers.

Christy sometimes suppresses her own aggressive tendencies to avoid antagonism from others. As a result, she appears diplomatic and non-aggressive. Despite this mild appearance, however, Christy has a strong need to control her environment.

One way in which she exerts this control is by requiring adherence to mutually accepted rules and standards. If this is not enough to achieve control, Christy resorts to indirect forms of control, including carefully developed plans to obtain the results she desires by controlling the conditions of the work environment. Or, she gathers as much information as possible to support her position, using the facts to override the arguments of others. This sometimes backfires, when she finds herself mired in details and misses the "big picture."

In a pressure situation, Christy is something of a worrywart. She can hold things up unnecessarily, seeking an unrealistic level of certainty or perfection. This can be annoying to others and troublesome to Christy herself.

Not only does Christy value her own analytical abilities, she also may judge others by this standard. She enjoys learning and finding beauty in logical arguments. She takes considerable satisfaction in reasoning and analytical activities, holding educated individuals in high esteem. She respects those who think before they act and collect adequate information before making decisions. On the other hand, she is less tolerant of those who are highly emotional, impulsive in their decision-making, or aggressive in their interactions with others. Christy has a small group of close friends with whom she interacts comfortably. She is likely to put a lot of energy into maintaining her relationships with this select group.

Christy enjoys being valued as part of the team or work group. However, when it comes to getting things done, she generally prefers to function on her own, though within agreed-upon guidelines. She requires many explanations when undertaking a new activity to make sure that she gets it "right," in order to meet her own standards.

When approaching a new problem or decision, Christy is cautious. She carefully analyzes all the data she thinks is relevant, taking time to obtain any information she thinks is missing. Her conclusion, while logical, may not appear to follow conventional steps in reaching it. While using her intuition to help her reach a decision, she seeks to support that conclusion with objective facts. If she makes an incorrect choice, she may resist acknowledging that fact—choosing instead to search for more and more data in an effort to validate her position.

Christy is a special person who can buffer the emotions of others and provide stability and balance. Easy to get along with, she tolerates flexible schedules. Balance is very important to Christy: She does not function in the extremes or excesses of life, but walks solidly down the middle road, avoiding conflict and decisions on either side. She does not offend, does not call attention to herself, and quietly does what is expected of her without looking for credit.

Christy is more of a "learned leader" than a born leader and with proper motivation can rise to the top because of her outstanding ability to get along with everyone. Christy tends to hold back until asked and is never pushy. One of Christy's most admirable traits is her ability to stay calm in the midst of a storm. Being cool and collected, she backs up and waits a minute, then moves quietly in the right direction.

One reason Christy has so many friends is that she is a good listener. She would rather listen than talk and doesn't mind keeping quiet. She doesn't have to say a word while other people are spouting off when they're stressed or troubled.

Christy is indirect in her style of communicating. She is very attentive to what others say and usually seeks out more information where necessary, but she doesn't like small talk. Christy is not tolerant of salespeople who can't speak intelligently and confidently about their products. Proposals that are messy, or not well thought out, can lose you the sale. Present traditional, conservative solutions. New ideas need support with factual evidence. If you don't know an answer, tell her you'll get back to her rather than guess. Don't wing it, because Christy tends to be very good at logical analysis of facts, and one wrong guess can lose her confidence.

Mastery – Adapting to Your Customer

Identifying Style

The descriptions of Doreen, Irving, Stephen, and Christy give you some good clues for identifying people's preferred styles. Most people are a blend of styles, and it's a good bet this will hold true with your customers. So, as you read the identifying information coming up, be prepared to find that your customer or prospect does several behaviors from each of the charts. That's fine—just see if you can determine which are the most *prevalent* styles. As you practice this, it will assist you in adapting your presentation to your customer.

You can easily identify a customer's primary behavioral style by observing two conditions. First, are they outgoing or reserved? Second, do they focus on the activities that need to be done (and these include final results of those activities) or do they focus on the people who will be involved?

An easy and clear way to chart this to assist you in identifying primary styles can look like the following.

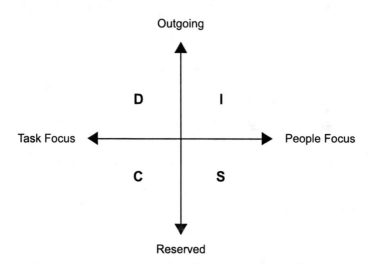

Using the chart as an example, if the person you're meeting with focuses on the tasks that need to happen and he comes across as very outgoing, he would likely be a "D" behavioral style. A customer who comes across as reserved and focuses on the people she works with is likely to be an "S" behavioral style. Let's say you meet someone new and while he is outgoing, he talks about both the activities that need to take place and the people he works with. This person is likely a "D" and "I" combination.

Another way to hone in on a customer's style is to choose words that accurately describe their behavior.

High "D" behaviors may be described with these words:

Ambitious	Argumentative	Blunt
Bold	Decisive	Demanding
Impatient	Stubborn	Tenacious

High "I" behaviors may be described with these words:

Animated	Charming	Cheerful
Compelling	Energetic	Enthusiastic
Expressive	Optimistic	Self-assured

High "S" behaviors may be described with these words:

Agreeable	Calm	Cooperative
Gentle	Helpful	Humble
Loyal	Patient	Predictable

High "C" behaviors may be described with these words:

Analytical	Cautious	Considerate
Diplomatic	Exact	Incisive
Meticulous	Private	Thoughtful

You may also notice several other aspects that give you clues to the customer's style. For example, how they dress, how they talk, the kind of personal interaction they have, and what their work environment looks like.

How they dress:

D	I	S	C
Professional	Trendy	Informal	Conservative

How they talk:

D	I	S	C
Self-assured	Loudly	Evenly	Composed

Personal interactions:

D	I	S	C
Controlling	Feeling-focused	Friendly	Detached

Work Environment:

D	I
Efficient and formal	Cluttered and friendly
S	**C**
Relaxed and personal	Organized and functional

Key Opportunities for Adapting to Your Customer

There are four major points in the sales process where you may find adapting to be most beneficial. These are: *initial contact, diagnosing the customer's needs, making presentations,* and *obtaining commitment or closing.*

Of course, with the initial contact, you will need to quickly identify the customer's style and then adapt. If you can't identify their style, then just act as you normally would on a sales call and adapt as you learn more. The fact is, **as you become more adept at this, you will be able to identify your prospect's style almost at first glance.**

However, as with any new skill, learning to assess and adapt takes practice. Practicing with your friends and family first will allow you to gain experience and make your mistakes in situations where they won't have a lot of repercussions. It's much better to make initial errors with people who love you unconditionally than with customers or potential customers.

And cut yourself some slack. Making the wrong judgment about a customer's style at an early stage of the sales process may temporarily put you off track for closing the sale, but it's not likely to cause permanent damage to the relationship, especially when you course-correct later.

Always pay attention to how you're being received. Watch for clues that you have evaluated the customer's style incorrectly so you can refine and adjust. After a while, you will find yourself becoming quite adept at classifying and adapting to your customers.

Initial Contact

You've already had a phone conversation or two with the prospect, so you've used their vocabulary to form a preliminary sense of their style. You walk in the door, shake hands, glance around the office, note how they're dressed. You literally have enough information to validate or revise your classification. Based on all of this, you can now tailor your behavior to start gaining the sale.

High "D" Style
- Keep socializing relatively brief and get directly to the point, for example: "My reason for this meeting is to respond to your interest in..."
- Keep your conversation businesslike.
- Respond to their key task-focused needs.
- Inquire about their goals and objectives.
- After talking business, depart without delay.

High "I" Style

- Introduce yourself first; don't be shy.
- Engage in casual, warm, friendly conversation.
- Focus on their feelings and aspirations. For example, say, "It seems that you feel strongly about..."
- Allow them time to talk about their ideas and people, and let them be the center of attention.
- Find out who their heroes are and whose business opinions they respect and admire; check out their bookcase very thoroughly to learn about their interests.

High "S" Style

- Display a sincere interest in them as a person, finding areas of common involvement; be candid and open.
- Focus on developing trust, friendship, and credibility.
- Be information oriented, low pressure, and people focused. For instance, ask, "How are things going for you and with business lately?"
- Move along in an informal, slow manner.

High "C" Style

- Get down to business in a diplomatic and task-focused manner.
- Be careful not to offend them or invade their privacy. (Do not mention that you've created a dossier on them.)
- Let them be the "expert." Ask indirect questions, drawing out their thoughts and ideas.
- Follow up your personal contacts with a letter recapping details of the conversation.

Diagnosing Needs

Wouldn't it be nice if every prospect knew just what they wanted or needed and could articulate it clearly? Not likely to happen. You need to know how to approach learning what prospects need so that you keep moving with them toward the close.

High "D" Style

- Be clear, specific, brief, and to the point.
- Ask about their goals and objectives, what they want to accomplish, what is happening now, and how they would like to see it changed.
- Focus on "what" questions, not "how" questions. For example, ask, "What's your number one goal at this time?"
- If timelines exist, get these into the open as related to end results or objectives.
- If they ask you questions, provide direct answers.

High "I" Style

- Ask open-ended questions that allow them to reveal more about their motivating concerns. "Could you expand on that?" is a good question to ask.
- Keep the interviewing process friendly, and remember that you're not here to interrogate them.
- Don't hurry the discussion; listen for both facts and feelings.
- Allow them plenty of opportunity to talk about things that are bothering them.
- Lead them gently into a more thorough awareness of their pain and its implications—they won't do it for themselves because it's too uncomfortable for them.
- Do your best to eliminate any inconsistencies in their thinking, or it will come back to haunt you.
- Work to help them come to the conclusion that there needs to be prompt action.
- Make time for relating/socializing throughout the meeting you have together, in person or via phone.

High "S" Style

- Exhibit genuine sincerity and include questions that focus on insuring stability for both project and relationship. For example, ask, "Would things be more stable if...?"

- Create a non-threatening environment for them. Don't push or make them feel that they are getting the third degree.
- Show that you are "actively" listening by asking detail-oriented follow-on questions to the information they provide you.
- Allow plenty of time to explore their feelings and to understand the emotional side of the situation as well as the technical and business needs.
- Recognize that they tend to keep many of their feelings to themselves by stating tentatively what they mean. Draw them out through specific questioning and reflective listening. For example, say, "This is what I heard you say..." and then ask, "Is that what you meant?"
- Patiently draw out personal goals and work with them to help achieve these goals.
- When you disagree, gently discuss personal opinions and feelings.

High "C" Style

- Approach the interview from a practical, logical manner.
- Stay on task; minimize small talk.
- Ask lots of questions and make sure your questions show a clear direction. You might segment your questions into three parts and tell them in advance how you're going to ask the questions.
- Include probes that allow them to express their knowledge, objectives, apprehensions, and strategies to the degree they desire. For instance, ask, "What have you found to be the most logical...?"
- If disagreeing, ask for clarification about specific facts.
- Ignore critical comments they make, but make sure they are not disguised questions that require a response, such as, "Are you sure that's the best approach?"
- All questions they ask are important to them—do not ignore questions that may seem irrelevant.

Presenting

When you've gotten to the point of making your presentation, these keys will keep you in the best position to move toward a successful close.

High "D" Style
- Use a general strategy that focuses on their goal of personal control and minimizes their fear of being taken advantage of.
- Discuss the expected results and make sure these results are consistent with what they have told you they want to accomplish.
- Make sure that they will maintain control as any problems are solved.
- Use feature and benefit statements that emphasize efficiency, profits, savings. For instance, you could say, "Our product/service has produced among the most profitable results in the field."
- Keep the presentation short and brisk, making sure your answers to their questions are brief and to the point.
- Stay on track and ensure that you obtain agreement with facts and ideas.
- Come prepared with all requirements, objectives, support material, etc., in a well-organized "package" with an executive summary up front, details in the back.
- To influence decisions, provide alternate actions and probabilities of their success.
- If they act as if they are restless, if they get blunt, sarcastic, critical, or fault-finding, lighten up on the pressure.

High "I" Style
- Plan your presentation to show how using your company can increase the prospect's level of social influence, while reducing their concerns about social rejection.

- Use feature and benefit statements that show how the customer can look good and save effort. For instance, say, "With our product/service, there'll be fewer worries and details for you to handle."
- Keep the pace fast-moving and remain relaxed.
- Provide ideas for transferring talk to action.
- Propose your solution with stories and illustrations that relate to the customer's company and their goals.
- Allow plenty of time, and minimize discussions about details.
- Use testimonials to positively influence decisions.
- Pay direct (and genuine) compliments to them as an individual.
- Never put them down in front of subordinates.

High "S" Style

- Research how your company will provide support for them and their group or organization. Your plan must emphasize how it will be steadying, stabilizing, and simplifying for their existing relationships and practices.
- Clearly define roles and goals and their place in the plan.
- Present your case softly, non-threateningly.
- Use statements that emphasize harmony and steadiness. For example, state, "The most common comment from people using our product/service is..." (Pause) "They have been content with what we have done for them and their people."
- Present ideas or departures from status quo in a non-threatening manner; give them a chance to adjust.
- Emphasize how their actions will minimize their risk.
- Describe your approach as "tested and verified."
- Provide guarantees that any actions will involve a minimum of risk.
- Show the human side of your proposal.
- Have them make periodic decisions throughout the presentation.

- Where possible, offer ongoing support. For example, say, "I can understand how you feel; I might feel the same way if I were in your shoes. On the other hand, realistically speaking..." If they seem reluctant to buy, you may need to dig for specifics about their real source of concern and then address that by offering support.
- Compliment the way they are regarded by other people, their relationship skills, their ability to get along with others.

High "C" Style

- Prepare your "presentation" in advance—be systematic, exact, and organized.
- Make sure your research assures accuracy and appeals to their concern for quality.
- Prepare a detailed and technical presentation.
- Be primed to address your company's track record, including why it is a logical investment for the client to make.
- Be prepared to provide any explanations in a patient and thorough manner.
- Be straightforward and direct; stick to business.
- Describe the process that you will follow, and provide an outline of how that process will produce the results they seek. Ask questions to help them give you the right information.
- Give reassurance that no surprises will occur.
- Provide a written copy of your presentation.
- Back up your claims with solid, tangible, factual evidence that what you say is true and accurate.
- Build your credibility by listing pros and cons to any suggestion you make.
- Draw out and respond to their most pressing questions.
- Support their dependence on logic by providing additional evidence to reassure them.
- Avoid gimmicks.

- Take time to answer all their questions about structure and guidance.
- Be sure to establish target times and deadlines.

Obtaining Commitment

Everything you have done with the prospect has brought you to this stage of the process. Nonetheless, it's not a sale until there is a final agreement. Here's how to carry through on the momentum you have already gained.

High "D" Style
- Quickly highlight their key options. Acknowledge that the decision is theirs to make. For instance, say, "It seems that your real options are.... Which do you think would work best for you right now?"
- Provide key alternatives and choices for making their decisions.
- If the prospect makes a statement you disagree with, disagree with the facts not with the person.
- Motivate and persuade by referring to objectives and results.
- They will probably be blunt. You remain objective.
- Demonstrate your genuine desire to support their quest for added results. For example, you can ask, "What's the single bottom-line issue you need to have addressed with this product/service?"
- Confirm their authority by providing two to three options, and let them make the decision.
- Ask for the order assertively.

High "I" Style
- Use an upbeat approach to inspire them to action, such as, "Wow! Just think of how...!" Then, ask directly for the order so as to enable you to meet their needs.

- Accept their feelings or doubts. Use a lot of feeling statements, such as, "It's only natural you'd feel this way—many people would feel that way, too."
- To motivate them, offer incentives; they love to get special treatment.
- Remember that they act impulsively—heart over mind—which you may be able to leverage to your objective.
- Gain agreement on the specifics.
- Assure that they fully understand what they have bought and can demonstrate their ability to use it properly.
- Keep the close relaxed and friendly.

High "S" Style

- Detail how they can take practical action.
- Give them the nurturing and reassurance that you would give someone who is highly concerned about the purchase they are about to make.
- Seek a concrete commitment, since they may otherwise postpone a decision. You might say, "Since we have agreed on this, here is what you simply need to do so that we can work together to achieve your goal."
- Offer personal assurances that you will stand behind any decisions.
- Confirm without pushing or rushing them.
- Strive to maintain status quo.
- Assure them by being consistent, regular, and thorough in your communication.

High "C" Style

- Draw up a scheduled approach to implementing action with a step-by-step timetable; assure them there won't be surprises.
- Point out guarantees.
- Lay out a step-by-step approach to their goal.

- Provide detailed information and/or testimonials where your new ideas have been successfully implemented.
- Communicate full explanations before suggesting any changes to be made.
- If change is required, provide a detailed approach to implementing that change with specific information on proposed safeguards.
- Offer options and clarify their priorities in making a reality-based decision about your product or service.
- Support their consistent demand for logical actions. For example, you could say, "As you have noted, facts speak for themselves. And the facts in this situation indicate the logic of the decision to buy." Pause slightly and then ask, "Are you in agreement?"
- Give them time to verify your words and actions.
- Do not rush the decision-making process.
- Avoid doing anything that may personally threaten them.
- Confirm as a matter of course. Don't push; give them time to think. Offer documentation.
- Assure them of adequate service and follow-through. Be complete.
- Recognize that because of their demanding performance standards, they can be your best endorsement for future business.

The Bottom Line on Behavior

Though this may seem to be a lot to learn and integrate, you may be surprised just how fast your skill grows. Take a little time to think about the customers you have and where they fit in the DISC matrix. Consider how you have dealt with them and what has been particularly successful—or unsuccessful—with them. See how that all fits in what has been presented here.

The fact is, once you become familiar with these basic concepts, you will find you are able to categorize a customer in as little as five seconds. From there you can immediately start adapting to their style and more effectively supporting their need. Imagine what that will do to your sales success record!

4: COMMUNICATION STYLE

It's your last call of the day. You've had a couple of previous calls with this potential customer. Both of you expect that you'll be delivering information that will influence their company to choose your company's products or a competitor's.

When you arrive, your competitor is walking out the door with a large smile on his face. As you start to give your presentation (one that you've given a hundred times before), the prospect interrupts you and asks questions that you feel you've just answered. In fact, you've given her solid information about her questions. She tells you she's just not hearing the things that she wants to hear.

After walking her through the handouts you've provided, she still has a look of confusion on her face. Finally she says that she has another meeting and that she will call you later in the week to continue the conversation. The call never comes, your calls aren't returned, and you shortly find out that your competition wrapped up the deal. You know that your company's products are far superior to the competition and less expensive. What happened?

We Make Sense through Our Senses

Your only connection with the physical world is through your five senses—sight, sound, smell, taste, and touch—and it is through those senses that you receive communication.

There are two processes that take place as you learn to communicate. First, you absorb your world through your senses as you seek to comprehend what is happening to you and what is happening around you. Next, you take these sensory inputs and project them back out into the world using whatever understanding you've developed—what we'll refer to as a "frame of reference." Often these projections are overlaid with thoughts you've developed over time about how the world works and with emotions based on how you felt at the time of the experience.

You've Got a Code

Here's how this applies to selling. Let's say that you successfully close a sale. In this peak emotional moment all your thoughts and emotions are coded into what you see, what you hear, and how you feel. The next time you're in a situation, you reenact (or project) the previous close. If it is again successful and you continue to do it, you have established a habit pattern or rule about how to close sales. People often narrow their channels of communication and continually play the same "motion picture" every time they are faced with a closing situation.

Across from the table is your customer. They are doing the same thing you are doing. They code an experience as a successful purchase. Eventually you will run into a customer who has coded a successful purchase very differently from your habit patterns of a successful close and your close will not work. You walk away confused because you always close sales when you play this particular "motion picture." Except, this time you didn't.

A critical part of communication is decoding your customer's approach to a successful purchase and comparing it to your approach for a successful sale. If the codes match, then there is a high likelihood that you will close the sale. If they don't match, you might as well be speaking a foreign language.

> *"Communicating carries with it a responsibility...to get the information from inside of us to the other person in a way that they can receive it."* – John-Roger, Inside Insight

When influencing your customers, your job is to take the information about your company, your products/services, and your ability and communicate it to your customers in a way that makes "sense" to them. In order to do that effectively, you need to understand how they *perceive* the world (i.e., through which senses they receive information).

How will you know if you're not doing your job? You will:

- Fail to consider anyone's viewpoint except your own
- Attach to your ways of viewing the world and assume that your customer has the same process
- Have a sense of urgency that is different from your customer's
- Send incomplete messages or use the wrong sensory channel (visual, verbal, etc.) to communicate clearly

According to George Bernard Shaw, *"The greatest problem in communication is the illusion that is has been accomplished."*

Making Sense of the World

Though you notice the world around you by using all your senses—seeing, hearing, feeling, tasting, and smelling—generally, one is the dominant way of experiencing things. Then when you take a sensory experience into your conscious or unconscious awareness, it is coded by your imagination, emotions, and mind. During this coding process, you attempt to make meaning of your sensory experience. Your current and future actions depend on the meanings you create in this process. In a sense, you create emotional word pictures.

Your thought process produces words that communicate the meanings of your perceptions. Over time, you choose words that reflect your experiences and the senses that you used to code the information. This is when you may develop a preference for one sense or another, depending on the experience.

For example, let's say you're on a beach, waves lapping on the shore, and you're observing a beautiful sunset that is emotionally stirring. As you are moved by this experience, you will have hardwired it inside of you. If you are visually oriented and an individual asks you if you have ever enjoyed a spectacular sunset, you will be able to describe in extraordinary detail the sunset that you visually coded in your mind. You will also make extensive use of visual words in describing the sunset.

If you are more auditory—sounds make more of an impression on you—you might describe how beautiful the waves sounded as they washed over the sand and gently flowed back away from you.

On the other hand, the sunset could have elicited strong emotional feeling within you. Your description would have a greater number of feeling or kinesthetic words: "It was very moving. I felt awed."

Your customer's language is a useful indicator of their experience when making a buying decision. The type of words they use will tell you, quite explicitly, what they want to see, hear, feel, taste, or smell. **Your ability to describe the key benefits of your product or service in language that matches their preferences will create the greatest impact on the customer.** This is true, first, because you will be using words that most strongly motivate the customer. And second, because it will allow the information to go into their awareness un-translated.

Translation from one sense to another is risky, as something is always lost in the translation. Often this "something" is the emotional impact the words would have on the customer. This is important because information merely delivers data. Emotional impact *moves to action.*

If your customer prefers visual descriptions and you make your presentation using auditory (sound) words, your customer will need to translate your description to match his preferences. While what you want is for the customer to receive the full impact of your well-crafted presentation, in fact you're asking him to do some mental gymnastics that will partly—or completely—distract him from the motivational impact of your message.

Consider this example of a common statement that might be made in a normal, day-to-day sales conversation. It illustrates how you can match another person's sensory preferences.

You're having a conversation with one of your customers. You've extensively gone over the benefits of your product, and he responds, "I was looking over your proposal, and it shows a number of interesting things that have not previously been brought to light."

Your matching response will be one of the following:

- "It certainly looks like a good idea to me. How does it look to you?"
- "It certainly sounds like a good idea to me. What do you have to say about it?"
- "It certainly feels like a good idea to me. How do you feel about it?"

Each response generally has the same structure: agreement and a question back to the customer. However, two of them would not have the same impact as the third.

Since your customer used the words "show" and "brought to light," the first response—which is couched in visual terms—would be the best one to use. It most closely matches the way the customer is communicating about his experience using specific visual words, and this response will move you forward on the track toward the sale. The others might not—or at least, not as effectively.

Here's how you can identify and communicate more effectively with your customers based on their sensory style.

Visuals

People who use their visual sense want to communicate using visual words and references. For example, they would like you to *focus* so you can *see* their point of *view*. They would like you to provide a *clear overview* of your product or service and then *highlight* the details.

Do you prefer your visual sense over the others? Do you see pictures in your mind's eye? Can you easily play back a movie of past experiences and accurately detail what each person is looking at? Can you visualize how you want the future to look? If you answered yes to any of these questions, you'll probably unconsciously use language that mirrors this viewpoint.

In conversations, visuals use terms that represent seeing. For example, "I get the picture," "I see what you mean," "That's clear to me."

Colors are important to visuals—in fact, the color of their room may impact them emotionally. If your product comes in various colors, watch the expression on your customer's face as he looks at the colors available. Without saying a word, he will communicate what he sees working or not.

When asking questions to understand customers' needs, make sure you take notes when they express their point of view, as it tends to be the only point of view they will consider. They will compare the experience of working with you and all previous sales professionals. They might make quick judgments about how you look, how you're dressed, whether you have lint on your clothing or not. All of these things, sometimes unseen by those less visual, have an impact on their decision to work with you.

Below are additional comments that may reveal that someone is a visual:

That's clear to me.
Can you picture that?
I want to get a better perspective.
I see what you mean.
That's a horse of a different color.
Let's focus in on this.

Now I see the light.
Do you see how clear it is?
That's a really bright idea.
Let's focus in on that point of view.
We must keep that in perspective.
Let me give you an example of this.
I want you to see something.
Let's take the long view.
That's a colorful way of putting it.

When describing your product or service to a visual person, it is critical that you put your benefit statements in visual terms. To assist you, below is a collection of words that are visually focused. Take your standard benefit statements and light them up with visual terms. Remember, though, that making them too bright will discolor the benefit.

An eyeful	Eye-opening
Appears to me	Expose
At a glance	Flash
Beam	Flashed on
Beyond a shadow of a doubt	Focus
Bird's-eye view	Get the scope of
Blinded by	Get perspective on
Brighten up	Glimpse
Bring into focus	Glittering
Catch a glimpse of	Graphic
Clear-cut	Hazy idea
Clearly written	Horse of a different color
Colorful	Illuminating
Cloud	Illustrate
Dim view	In light of
Enlightening	Imaginative
Eye to eye	Imagine this scene

I get the picture	Plainly see
It's clear that	Pretty as a picture
Looks like	Preview
Lost/gained focus on	Project the image
Make a scene	Revealing
Mental image	Scope out
Mental picture	See
Mind's eye	See to it
Naked eye	Shortsighted
Outlook	Showing off
Outshines	Sight for sore eyes
Paint a picture	Spectacle
Paint the town	Sunny
Panoramic	Take a peek
Perspective	Tunnel vision
Photographic memory	Vibrant
Picture	Vivid
Picture-perfect	

Auditories

Those whose dominant sense is hearing are different from visuals. They don't come from the world of images; theirs is a world of sounds. They don't need to see whether something is in order; they need to hear if it is. They attach meaning to life patterns by hearing dialogue and adding narration.

Are you the kind of person who can remember conversations word for word? When you're negotiating on the phone do you easily recall what was agreed to and what wasn't? Do sharp or loud sounds interrupt your thoughts? If you answered yes to any of these questions, you'll probably use language that harmonizes with sound words.

Auditories often talk to themselves. They may have difficulty making choices until they have talked things out in their mind. If you're speaking with an auditory and they stop talking and break eye contact, pause. Let them have their internal discussion, and when they look at you again, ask this question: "Now that you've had a chance to mull that over, please voice your opinion." Listen carefully to what they say, as the words will be spoken unedited. They will literally "speak their mind."

In conversations, auditories use terms that represent hearing. For example, "That rings a bell," "I hear you," and "Please call me."

Sounds are important to auditories. In fact, music is what balances them emotionally. If your product makes unusual sounds, let the auditory know this in advance when you demonstrate it. You don't want them unpleasantly surprised—you want them coming away from the demo with a harmonious experience.

Auditories will hear you quite well and often indicate this through gesture cues. The most common of these is pointing to their ear when telling you to explain something in more detail. Don't be offended; this is a simple request for more information, not a stall.

Below are additional comments that auditories may make when communicating with you:

Tell me how you like this model.
Can we talk?
Keep your ear to the ground.
Can you hear what I mean?
This rings true for me.
That's clear as a bell.
Hey, listen to this.

Sounds good to me.
Talk to me.

When describing your product or service to someone who is auditory, it is critical that you put your benefit statements in auditory terms. To assist you, below is a collection of words that are hearing focused. Take your standard benefit statements and accent them with auditory terms. Be careful, though; too many of these terms in your statements will muffle the benefits.

Accent	Hold your tongue (also
Afterthought	kinesthetic)
Alarm	Idle talk
Amplify	Inquire into
An earful	Keynote speaker
Blabbermouth	Listen to
Call on me	Loud and clear
Chatting	Manner of speaking
Chord	Muffle
Click	Note
Clear as a bell	Power of speech
Clearly described	Purrs like a kitten
Compose	Outspoken
Describe in detail	Rap session
Earshot	Rattle
Express yourself	Resonate
I'm hearing you	Ring
Give an account of	Rings a bell
Give me your ear	Say
Growl	Screech
Harmonize	Shout it out
Hear	Sing
Heard voices	Sizzling
Hidden message	Sound

State your purpose
Static
Symphony
Tattletale
To tell the truth
Tongue-tied
Tuned in/out

Turn up the volume
Unheard of
Utterly
Voiced an opinion
Well informed
Within hearing range

Kinesthetics

Do you make decisions by how the situation feels to you? Do you need to retrace your steps to remember where you placed the contract? Do you like to have everything within reach of your desk? If you answered yes to any of these questions, you'll have a strong sense that you're a kinesthetic.

In the United States, olfactory and gustatory senses (smell and taste) are not favored. In fact, much of American advertising is aimed at getting rid of odors and bad smells. In some other countries, languages are much richer in that they have words for smells and tastes that make many distinctions that do not even exist in English. However, both smell and taste can be powerful stimuli and they are part of the kinesthetic system.

If your customer is kinesthetic, you want to help them get a feel for the benefits, grasp key points, and move forward with the investment. They may also have a need to sink their teeth into your ideas, chew over the facts you've presented, and sniff out any problems. As long as you come up with a tasty solution, they'll follow your train of thought.

Below are additional comments that kinesthetics may make when communicating with you:

Tell me how you feel about it.
I have a grasp on the key points.
Can we move forward?
I feel a little off base about your idea.
I don't want to dredge up old problems.
Help me get a handle on this.

When describing your product or service to these people, it is critical that you put your benefit statements in kinesthetic terms. To assist you, below is a collection of words that are feeling focused. Take your standard benefit statements and lightly salt them with kinesthetic terms. Be careful; dropping too many terms into your statements will come across as heavy-handed.

Adorable	Get a handle on
All embracing	Get a load of this
All washed up	Get in touch with
Boils down to	Get the drift of
Bracing	Get your goat
Casual	Gripping
Chip off the old block	Handy
Cold, hard facts	Hand in hand
Comfy	Heavy
Come to grips with	Heavy-handed
Control yourself	Heated argument
Cool, calm, and collected	Hold it
Crisp	Hold on
Cushiony	Hothead
Down home	Huggable
Exhaustive	In-depth
Feels good to me	If it feels right
Firm foundation	Keep your shirt on
Floating on air	Knee slapping
Follow your train of thought	Lay your cards on the table

Lightheaded (also visual)
Moment of panic
Moving
Not following you
Oven fresh
Peaceful
Placid
Powerful feeling
Pull some strings
Roomy
Serene
Sharp as a tack
Silky
Slipped my mind

Snug
Smooth operator
Soothing
Start from scratch
Stiff upper lip
Stuffed shirt
Sweeping
Too hot to handle
Too much of a hassle
Topsy-turvy
Uncut
Underhanded
Velvety

I've tested several thousand sales professionals over the last 20 years to determine if they were primarily visual, auditory, or kinesthetic. The vast majority (over 65%) were kinesthetics. For non-salespeople I've tested, the vast majority are visual. Do you grasp the impact of this? There's a good chance your natural language may not be the same as your customers'. However, now you have the resources to adapt and make your case far more powerfully.

Cerebrals

What about people who don't use many sensory-based words in their communication? Occasionally, I'll have a customer who uses buzzwords and not much else. It's almost as if he uses words to separate his sensory connection with the world, or uses them as protection from the world. Cerebrals have a thick filter of language between their perceptions and their responses. Here's an example of something a cerebral might communicate:

Memo to Associates:

In benchmarking our company's performance against a peer group since our recent re-engineering, we realize that further rightsizing is in order to achieve the efficiencies needed to return to our core competencies. To ensure that this continues to be a high-performance workplace, we will begin outsourcing our human resources functions and convert other departments into cross-functional teams. A paradigm shift is necessary if we are to remain a learning organization in an era of discontinuous change. Our vision is that you empowered intrapreneurs, along with our fast-growing contingent work force, will think out of the box as we implement total quality processes. Our change management expert will contact you to explain our utilization of 360-degree feedback as part of our transformation to a pay-for-performance model.

Yours in excellence,

John Leader

Below are additional comments that cerebrals may make when communicating with you:

I understand what you mean.
I thought last night was really nice.
How much are you interested?

What these statements have in common is a lack of juice. There's nothing to latch on to. You can't see clearly what they are communicating. So, you'll need to coax out a deeper level of communication. It's as easy as asking them if they can be more specific about what they've just said.

Knowing Who's a What

Identifying the preferred sense your customer uses is literally as easy as listening for the words they use. If you're a visual, you can watch what they do when communicating with you. Visuals have a tendency to maintain strict eye contact while you're speaking. Auditories will tend to cock one ear in your direction, if only to hear you more clearly. Kinesthetics will tend to use hand gestures frequently when speaking.

Personal space is also important. Visuals will want to keep you at a distance because it's much more difficult to take in the whole picture when you're standing close. Auditories have a slightly smaller personal space, if only to reduce any external static that may rattle the communication. Kinesthetics have the smallest personal space of all. In fact, touching each other is part of kinesthetic communication.

Knowing When to Use Which Mode

Some people use only one type of sensory specific communication. Others use all three and may mix their descriptions of what they are working to accomplish in an attempt (conscious or unconscious) to make sure that at least part of their message gets through. To give your message the greatest impact, your job is to quickly identify and then adapt your communication to the primary, if there is one.

If there does not seem to be a primary, then respond to them in the mode they are using in stating their needs. That is, if they're using visual words to describe what they want to accomplish, then you will need to use visual words as you describe how you're going to help them accomplish their goal.

If your client keeps asking you to tell them more, and you've already given them the kitchen sink, it may be time to rethink your evaluation of them. They may be telling you this because you're speaking different languages. They may be using visual terms and you may be using auditory terms. If you're not careful the conversation could sound like this.

Customer: "What else can you show me?"
Salesperson: "I've just told you everything that I can about our service."
Customer: "I still don't have a good focus on this."
Salesperson (exasperated): "I don't know what more to say."
Customer: "Well, you're going to have to show me more than this."
Salesperson: "Perhaps you're not hearing me."
Customer: "I hear you just fine. So what I'm going to do is show you the door. Goodbye."

Not a happy ending for either the salesperson or the customer. And yet some simple observation of the words chosen by the customer and some small adjustments by the salesperson could have easily resulted in a lifelong customer.

When your communication is not in sync, customers have to translate what you said. Remember, something is always lost in the translation. In this case, it was the customer's final vision of having made a successful purchase.

A key area many salespeople forget to ask about is the customer's buying process. You might ask them these three questions:

1. What is the first thing you consider when making a buying decision?

2. What is the second thing?
3. What is the third thing?

Jot down specific notes as they respond to these questions. They may tell you that they consider: visual information, visual information, and kinesthetic information. **This is like a combination lock to their buying process and they have given you the numbers.** Your closing statement needs to be synchronized to their statements. You would give them a visual benefit or closing statement, followed by another visual statement, and finally a kinesthetic statement.

Experiment with this. You might be amazed at how effective a technique this simple three-sentence process can be.

Frames of Reference

The following may just be some of the most valuable knowledge you will ever receive for enhancing your sales career. It may also be some of the most challenging. Take your time, because you will be dealing with individuals' perceptual filters. Everything presented so far is part of a larger context or what we can call points of view or frames of reference. All your communication and sales relationships occur in this context and influence whether your business dealings will succeed...or fail.

The Frame Game

The process of packaging communication is called framing. Take a moment and, in your mind's eye, visualize the painting "Mona Lisa." Now step back from the picture for a moment and conjure up an image of the "Mona Lisa" with a steel polka-dot frame around it. Does this new frame seem appropriate? In your mind, how does this new frame affect your perception of this very famous painting? Is part of you cringing at the thought?

If you consider "Mona Lisa" as a message or communication, the way it is framed impacts how that message is received by the viewer. Framed appropriately, the message communicates the artist's intent. Framed inappropriately, the message loses the meaning intended. Your ability to correctly frame your messages will impact the success of each sales call.

What are the rules for framing the "Mona Lisa"? Some of them might include:

- Paintings from the early 1500s need to be in frames that also represent that time period.
- Frames need to be in the Italian style.
- Frames need to be made of wood.

Obviously, a steel polka-dot frame made in the 21st century doesn't match these rules. Taking a masterful work of art and putting it in a whimsical frame would transform how the painting was received from masterpiece to cartoon. So, too, can your message be influenced by how you frame it.

Since these rules reside in our thought process and beliefs, we could easily be rattled by a frame we perceive as inappropriate. Depending on the sales situation you're in, some statements are appropriate to make and some are inappropriate; some appropriate actions may be humorous and others serious.

Every corporate environment has its own rules about appropriate and inappropriate communication. You may find yourself in situations where you don't have enough information to figure out what is appropriate. In these situations, you may project previous successful behavior that may work or just might result in disaster.

What if you find yourself in a situation where you need to do something, but all of the other parties are expecting a different response? How would you handle it? Here is one example of masterful selling (courtesy of Samuel Clemens):

On a warm, sunny, summer Saturday afternoon, Tom Sawyer has been sentenced to whitewash 30 yards of board fence. Tom's friends are coming along to go swimming and stop to make fun of him.

"Hello, old chap, you got to work, hey?"

"Why, it's you, Ben! I warn't noticing."

"Say I'm going a-swimming, I am. Don't you wish you could? But of course you'd druther work wouldn't you? Course you would!"

Tom contemplated the boy a bit, and said:

"What do you call work?"

"My, ain't that work?"

Tom resumed his whitewashing, and answered carelessly: "Well, maybe it is, and maybe it ain't. All I know is, it suits Tom Sawyer."

"Oh come, now, you don't mean to let on that you like it?"

The brush continued to move.

"Like it? Well, I don't see why I oughtn't to like it. Does a boy get a chance to whitewash a fence every day?"

That put the thing in a new light. Ben stopped nibbling his apple. Tom swept his brush daintily back and forth—stepped back to note the effect—added a touch here and there, criticized the effect again—Ben watching every move and getting more and more interested, more and more absorbed.

Presently he said:

"Say, Tom, let me whitewash a little."

By the middle of the afternoon, the fence had been painted and Tom had collected a fee from each of his friends for the privilege of participating in the experience. Tom had reframed whitewashing the fence from a detestable chore into a chance of a lifetime for which people were willing to pay to *enjoy* doing.

Reframing: Taking Control & Rewriting the Rules

Two elements of any frame include: the emotional word pictures and the sensory-based words they use. *In the sales calls where I've had the opportunity to observe (including my own), about 80% of objections were created by the salesperson. Why? Because we have communicated in a way that doesn't match the perceptions or beliefs of the customer.*

Consider the concept of *reframing* as a method to change the perceptions of the customer. You may have heard it this way: "If your customer hands you lemons, turn them into lemonade." This statement implies that if you squeeze the objection and add sugar to change the taste, the customer may buy it. The reality is, they may be so used to this repackaging process that they automatically dismiss it.

A more elegant way is to take the perceived disadvantage and reframe it as an advantage. To do this, you must be very clear about the multiple meanings implied in any frame of reference.

Not a Bigger Picture, a Better Picture

In the 1984 presidential debates between Walter Mondale and Ronald Reagan, a key issue was Reagan's age. He was 78 years old. This issue kept coming up in remarks from the press, comments from columnists, etc. During the second debate, one of the panelists finally asked the question directly on national television. Ronald Reagan's response was:

"I will not make age an issue of this campaign. I am not going to exploit, for political purposes, my opponent's youth and inexperience."

The entire audience, including Walter Mondale, erupted in laughter. More importantly, this objection to his presidency never came up again.

Know the Rules

What were the rules in play before Reagan's response? Most people have rules about age: Older people are less flexible, less energetic. Other rules that may apply are that older people are often wiser, as they have more experience in the world.

Ronald Reagan had been working hard to create an image of being robust. Many of the photo opportunities he crafted for the press were of him chopping wood or riding horses at his ranch in Santa Barbara. Even that wasn't enough, as the question of his age surfaced again and again. The only way he could combat this was to reframe people's perception that he wasn't *old*; he was *wise and experienced.* He couldn't say this directly because it would easily be dismissed. However, he could say it by implication. And that is what he did during the debate.

Is the Objection Really Objectionable?

To get a sense of this technique, make a list of all of the objections that you hear in your sales calls. Then categorize them from most important to least important. Think about the rules or beliefs that are implied in the objection. What other rules might be logical or believable that are not being focused on? Now think about some ways to reframe these objections.

For example, if your company's balance sheet isn't the best in the world and your competitor is constantly telling your customers this, check your competitor's balance sheet carefully. With one of my customers, we found that their competitor didn't invest nearly as much in research and development as my customer. When we added in the same amount, the competitor's balance sheet looked much worse than my customer's. The salespeople were trained to use this information and provided with actual copies of both companies' balance sheets. Within a month, the competitor stopped using this sales argument.

Take 'Em by Surprise

Sometimes you need to reframe using behaviors that may seem paradoxical. Your communication may appear odd or illogical; however, it can break through resistance. This approach is designed to shift a person's perception of rules.

Here's how it works: If I say, "XYZ," and everyone responds "ABC," what happens if I say, "XYZ," and the person I'm speaking with (the salesman) suddenly says "QLM"? I've got to stop and try to make sense of what he has just said. It may require that I rewrite my rulebook for communication.

Here is a great example of this technique:

> *In the early years of copier sales, there was a large company that every copier salesperson in town called on. Everybody knew that the company was a prime candidate for copiers, yet the purchasing manager made every effort*

> to destroy any and every attempt to sell him one. He would do this by having his secretary bring in the salesperson's business card, which he would tear up into little pieces (XYZ). He then had the secretary give the pieces back to the salesperson. Every salesperson would leave either angry or dejected (ABC).
>
> One salesperson took a different approach. When the secretary returned with the torn-up business card, he asked her for a stapler. Puzzled, she gave him the stapler to use. He then stapled his card back together and asked the secretary to give the card back to the purchasing manager and tell him, "I think you will find our copiers much more durable than my business card." (QLM)This salesperson ended up with a new customer who bought several copiers from him.

Paradoxical reframing helps your client break out of crystalized ways of perceiving the world. It requires that you intentionally alter the components of the frame. You actually break the standard rules of communication. To do this effectively, you need to clearly understand the cultural rules of the customer's company.

If you break a communication rule that also violates a company's cultural rule, this will backfire on you. This is why we spend time assessing the corporate culture in building trust. Gift-giving may allow you to reframe some situations. In certain businesses/industries, gift-giving is an acceptable part of the sales process. However, when working with federal government employees, it not only is unacceptable, but could cause them to lose their job.

If you don't know the cultural rules, ask. Say something like, "I would guess that your company has certain guidelines you need to follow in order to implement my suggestions. Could you educate me on the specifics so that I don't run afoul and make a mistake?"

Not a Bigger Picture, a Bigger View of the Picture

The process of reframing creates a different viewpoint, much like enlarging the frame around a photograph. Suppose you were looking at a photo of a house in a frame with a very small image area. Expanding the frame might show you that the house was sitting in a field. Widening the frame would allow you to see that a forest surrounded the house and field. Every time you enlarge the frame, you have more information to work with. Enlarging the frame with your customer allows you to get a better perspective of their needs.

How might this work with a real customer? Let's say you have a customer tell you that she wants a laptop with a long battery life (four hours) and your offering only works for two hours. You don't know why she has this specification, so you ask. "I know that you have stated that you want a four-hour battery life; can you please tell me how you would be using the laptop?"

You discover that the customer takes long flights and uses the laptop extensively on the plane. A little further probing and an understanding of how planes are equipped might allow you to reframe the customer's perceptions.

On investigation, you find that she flies first class and that there is electric power to the seat. You could suggest that the smaller battery makes your laptop much lighter and that the addition of the power adaptor would still be lighter than the laptop that has four hours of battery life. If you expand the frame a little further, you find that she flies transatlantic several times a year. Even a four-hour battery would have limitations on a seven- to ten-hour flight. The adapter would allow her to work the entire flight if she wanted.

Every time you expanded the "How are you going to use the product" frame, you got more information that allowed you to reframe her perceptions.

What makes reframing such an effective tool of change is that once your prospect perceives the new alternatives, she cannot easily return to her previous perceptions of the world. If you help a customer know their perceptions, they are no longer bound by them. They now have the freedom to choose different alternatives—alternatives that you propose.

Your skill in communicating an appropriate frame of reference for your client will assist you in reducing the number of objections you mistakenly create. More importantly, it will help you close more sales.

Emotional Word Pictures

In the chapter on motivation, the term "emotional word pictures" was introduced. Specifically, these are statements that tie in feelings (emotion), specific sounds (words), and visuals (pictures). By paying close attention to the statements your customers use, you will gain clear keys for persuading them more effectively with emotional word pictures.

You may notice that they use industry-specific jargon, metaphors and similes and analogies. Metaphors, similes, and analogies are used to help explain how one thing that may be unfamiliar is something like another, possibly more familiar thing.

Make Sure You're Playing in the Same Stadium

Sometimes customers will use figures of speech that reflect their personal interests, such as sports. "We were fourth and ten and we needed to punch the ball over the goal line." "We really dropped the ball in that situation." Figures of speech that reflect war are also popular in business: "That idea blew up on us." The imagery of the language used shows us what's valued, what's feared, and what the speaker's rules of communication are.

Words have very specific meaning to the person using them, because they are drawn from that person's specific experience. That experience may be identical to one you've had, slightly different, or totally opposite.

Our biggest challenge in communication is assuming that we understand another person's experience and the specific words they are using to symbolize that experience. In other words, we assume the words or images they are using mean the same thing to us as they mean to them. For example: "You know, it was first and goal for us on the Barker deal. We had to run the Statue of Liberty play to fake out our competition. But we were able to make it into the end zone."

The statement above might make total sense to you if you're an American football fan. If you don't know much about football, you might have a sense of what's being said, but you probably are at a loss as to the real communication here.

What's more, from this kind of languaging we can be pretty confident that the rules of football are also the business rules this person would tend to follow. Clearly, he is also saying that he is not above trickery to accomplish his goals, so you would want to pay close attention to any sleight of hand during negotiations. Language is almost always very revealing, even when people try to hide behind the words being used.

Industry-Specific Imagery

Customers actually use multiple levels of communication. They have figures of speech for the industry they are in. Pharmaceutical industry metaphors might obviously be different from manufacturing metaphors. So, too, botanical medicinals metaphors might differ from patent medicine metaphors, even though both companies are in the broad industrial classification of pharmaceuticals.

Different companies in the same industry might have entirely different figures of speech based on the way their culture works. One company may have a hierarchical organizational structure and another might be team based that focuses on solving problems. The metaphors you hear being used by the people within these two companies might have significant differences.

The Personal Perspective

An individual's position in the company might cause differences in the type of metaphors used. For example, the VP of Sales might have very different metaphors than the CEO of the company—though they might both use the same industry- and company-specific metaphors.

And finally, an individual's personal figures of speech might be distinctive.

Just as our language is a reflection of our personal experiences, language also shapes what we think about and how we think about it. In sales, persuasion means using language a customer can relate to, to open opportunities for them to consider.

Being persuasive requires entering into the perceptual reality of your client, paying attention to the words they live by, and articulating your communication using words that are consistent with their metaphors.

Use the Imagery That Communicates to Your Customer

So, how do you enliven your language with vitalizing imagery that is consistent with the customer, their company, or their personal situation?

It Starts with Awareness

First, be aware of the way you currently use metaphors and imagery. Most people use them in everyday conversation, but may not be aware that they are using them. Often what they use is clichéd. For example, "The lights are on but nobody's home." You could use a different metaphor such as, "He's a few pickles short of a Happy Meal." The intent of the communication is the same; the metaphor is different and the difference will capture another person's imagination. If you can use metaphors that fit the customer's unique situation, so much the better.

Think about what you are selling. Is there a way to communicate the benefits of your product or service using the industry, company, position, or personal metaphors of your customer?

Consider the industry the customer is in. Read the industry trade journals to gain an awareness of industry buzzwords and metaphors already in use.

John was selling training to the management of a company that makes engineered lumber. Essentially, the customer's company takes a tree, chops the wood into small pieces,

soaks it in glue, and then runs the slurry through a
microwave press. The reconstituted wood that comes out
the other side is actually stronger than the original tree.

Here's how John pitched to this company's management:
"What we are going to do is help your managers break
their business units down into component parts, infuse
good business planning, and then bring it all together with
the heat and pressure of round-robin assessments."

The CEO of the company looked at John and said, "That'll
work." And the deal was closed.

Why was it that simple a sale? Because John used a
metaphor that the CEO was familiar with, one he could see,
one he knew was effective. He knew, on some level, that
the process John described would produce the results he
wanted for his company!

Avoid Culture Clash

Next consider the culture of the company. Read business reports
about the company; talk with people who are already doing
business with the company. What can they tell you about the
culture? If you've created a customer profile to ensure you connect
in order to build rapport, you may have already done this.

Professional Word Preferences

Consider the individual's position. Following is a list of occupation-
related words we have gathered from a variety of fields to give you
a sense of how language can be profession-specific without
necessarily relying on technical terms of the profession. Normally,
you will find that your customer will use words that relate to their

field, and these indicate preferences. Listen for them. The following list is only suggestive; there is no substitute for noticing the word preferences of your particular customer. You can then take these words and construct new and fresh metaphors.

Accountant

accounts	accrete	accurate
actuarial	adds up	amortize
analyze	cash flow	clients
conservative	conservator	depreciate
estimates	facts	figures
forms	inaccurate	invest
IRS	precise	projections
recoup	revenue	shelter
tax bracket	taxes	

Attorney

case	claim	complaint
defend	determine	disclaimer
document	evaluation	evidence
judge	jury	legal
malfeasance	plaintiff	procedures
trial		

Computer Engineer

analysis	crash	data
design	dimensions	entry
field	flow	generate
logic	model	proposal
report	structure	subroutine
test	verify	

Small Businessperson

cash flow	employees	expand
inventory	loss	profit
sales	taxes	turnover

If you're a stockbroker and have customers in many different professions, you might write out what you're going to say. For example, if your message has to do with the strength of a client's portfolio, in stockbroker terminology the message might be: "I've looked over your portfolio and think you should consider making a few changes because some of the items are technically weak."

While accurate and correct, that may not be the best wording to use for someone who's not a stockbroker. You might change this fundamental statement so that it more accurately reflects the needs of your customers. For an architect, you might say, "I've looked over your portfolio and see some need to make a few *structural* changes. There are other securities that will provide a better *foundation* for your long-term goals."

For a physician, it could be, "I've examined your securities and my *diagnosis* is that some minor *preventive surgery* will improve the long-term *health* of your portfolio."

The Environment Speaks Volumes

Finally, consider the individual's personal metaphor. What is in their office, hanging from the walls, sitting on their desk or credenza? Are there golf trophies or golfing pictures in the office? If so, what golf metaphors could you use to tie in what you are selling with their personal experience?

Think through the metaphors that you're going to use. You'll initially come up with clichés. Discard the first two things that come to mind. Taking the time to work on this will result in communication that reflects the other person's world, is fresh, and captures their imagination.

A word of caution is required, though. Be careful not to mix your metaphors with the client's. If the culture of your client includes many war metaphors and you discuss your product or service in terms of doves and flowers, they'll probably use the catapult to eject you from the building.

Concluding Thoughts on Communication

Effective communication in sales is much more than having a good command of the language or even being able to represent yourself clearly. It has to do with knowing what "sub-language" (visual, auditory, or kinesthetic) your customer speaks, how to frame your presentation to overcome objections, and what metaphors to employ so that your customer is persuaded by what you've said.

Sure, it takes practice to become effective at it. But then, see yourself hitting that hole-in-one, hear the ka-ching of the cash register, and feel the sun on your skin as you lie on that Caribbean beach reaping the reward you gave yourself for a great sales year.

5: PUTTING IT ALL TOGETHER

How and When to Apply What You've Learned

When I was a kid, I got a model airplane kit. I opened the box and laid out all the parts. I could identify many of the pieces and I knew what the finished product was supposed to look like. But I wasn't quite sure how to get from a box of parts to a model plane.

Fortunately, my kit had a set of instructions. They looked pretty complex at first glance, but as I got into the process, I found they actually made sense. They put everything into a larger context and showed how it all fit together.

That's what this chapter is: a set of instructions that gives the larger selling context and explains how to assemble the components to end up with more successful sales.

I didn't build my model plane in one sitting. It took a while. And my early efforts at gluing and assembly were pretty rough. While I got better with practice, my first model was not something I showed to many people.

How to Eat an Elephant

Learning these sales skills is a similar process. In fact, to shift metaphors, it's something like eating an elephant: You can't do it in one sitting, but you probably could do it if you were allowed to take one bite at a time over a period of weeks. So give yourself time to taste and digest all of this.

A word of caution: Be aware of becoming too enthused about what you notice when meeting with your customers. You may find that you begin to see and hear things about them that you've never been aware of before. In fact, you may notice so much more about them, their office, and your interaction with them that you forget to focus on your primary job, which is to sell your product or service. It's not unusual for the customer to say that they would like to place an order and you don't hear them because you're focused on their behavioral style or communication patterns.

The Key to Getting There

There is an old joke about a young musician in New York City carrying a violin case who rushes up to a policeman and says, "How do I get to Carnegie Hall?" The cop glances at the violin case and says, "Practice, practice, practice."

Every star performer, from musician to sports figure, will tell you that practice is the key to their success. I have clients whom I've shared these principles with, and they will tell you the same thing. Not because they particularly enjoyed the practice, but they sure enjoyed—and continue to enjoy—the results.

A Step at a Time

So, practice these skills first before starting to use them in a sales situation. Tackle just one or two at a time—there's a lot to learn and digest. The best place to practice them is at home or in social situations with friends and family. If you make a mistake and fall on your face, these people will still love you. And they will appreciate that you are giving them more quality attention. As you get more skilled, and especially as you keep your focus on compassion, you'll begin to notice that your friends and family respond to you differently—most likely in a more harmonious and agreeable way.

Once you've begun to feel comfortable with one of the skills, once it feels truly natural to you, then—and only then—start to use it in the sales environment. As you begin experimenting with it, be aware of how you do things differently and how the customer responds to you. The customer may or may not notice any differences. All of this depends on how comfortable you are with the skill and whether you are subtle with it.

Don't Discuss, Just Do It

Here's another hint: Don't discuss what you're doing with customers. They may not understand that the foundation of everything you've learned is compassion and, specifically, compassionate listening. If you discuss the specific skills, people often become very uncomfortable and self-conscious. For most people, it's a short mental leap from "They're trying to connect with me" to "They're attempting to manipulate me." As soon as a person feels like they're being manipulated—whether you're doing that or not—the dragons of resistance and revenge rear up.

You want to avoid this at all costs. It's very difficult to recover once a person has turned negative toward you. They will see each subsequent effort to regain trust as another manipulation attempt.

Take the time to learn and become comfortable with these subtle but powerful techniques. Once you are ready to start using them, be sure to do it carefully and keep to yourself what you're doing. Then go ahead and apply it in the larger context of the buying process.

The Buying Process

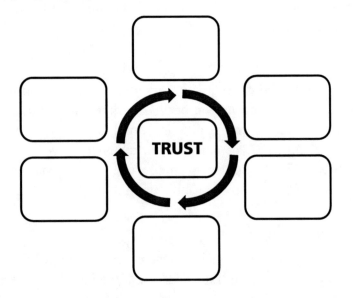

All the PeopleSavvy resources you've read about here can be applied at almost any point in your dealings with a customer. However, there are certain phases of the buying process where some techniques are more effective than they are at other times. In order to best understand this, however, you need to be aware of the dynamics of the buying process.

Most books on selling take an approach to the market consistent with what the *salesperson* experiences: Namely, the salesperson prospects, qualifies, presents, negotiates, and finally closes, with the end-result being a signed purchase order or contract. This is a standard approach that helps newer salespeople quickly get productive—it instructs on how to get to the goal of making the sale.

PeopleSavvy is different. Its focus is on building a genuine relationship with the buyer so the close of a sale is only a step along the road to creating continual sales, making larger sales, and gaining enthusiastic referrals. To accomplish this, you focus on the issues the *buyer* considers when making a purchase. **Your ability to understand the issues, influence the buyer's perception of issues, and earn the buyer's commitment is your measure of effectiveness. The sale is a natural by-product of this.**

The buying process is really a repeating cycle with clearly defined stages or steps. Modern research into buying behavior was first spelled out in a study titled "A Behavioral Theory of the Firm," published by Cyert and March in 1963. Since that time, literally hundreds of articles and books have been written about how people buy.

The Buying Process model you will be learning is based on the BUYGRID model published in *Industrial Buying Behavior and Creative Marketing* by Robinson, Faris, and Wind in 1967. While this model may not be as sophisticated as some used to describe organizational buying behavior, it is an accurate description of what happens—simple to understand and easy to relate to as you begin to integrate your PeopleSavvy skills.

Phase 1: Changing Environment
or
What influences do you need to know about that will affect how you serve your customer?

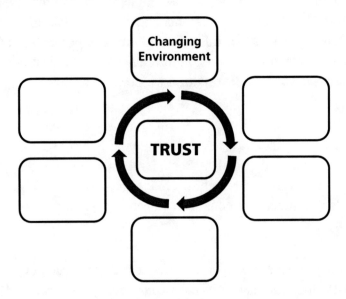

Change is a natural and integral part of business. Business is always in a state of change, whether from changes in demand, changes in the marketplace, changes in technology, changes in supply, changes in the competitor's product or service, changes in management, changes in workforce size, etc. Change impacts all businesses and the results they are working to achieve. Some of these changes cause the business to take action, and some don't. **Only when the environmental changes have sufficient consequences to overcome corporate comfort zones does a company take action.**

Know the Changes

What is important for you as a sales professional is to constantly be aware of how environmental changes affect the prospect so you know how to address their needs. To accomplish this, you need to gain understanding of both their internal and external changes.

Some internal environmental changes for a company are:
- Management changes, especially at the senior level
- Changes in missions and objectives of the organization
- Changes in strategies and policies of the organization
- Changes in short-range and long-range plans
- Changes in facilities (new, modernized, obsolete)
- Organizational change (downsizing, rightsizing, upsizing are all indications of this)

Some external environmental changes for a company are:
- Changes in perceptions or requirements of the prospect's customer base
- Increased or decreased competition
- Economic influences (inflation, recession, status quo)
- Population changes (aging of baby boomers, Gen-X, Gen-Y, etc.)
- Political or regulatory changes
- Technological changes (especially if these changes help the account create new products or services or make their current products or services obsolete)

The more awareness you have of what specifically is impacting the prospect's day-to-day operations, the better chance you have of establishing a relationship.

Know the Rules

Further influencing the corporate comfort zone are the rules by which the prospect must conduct business. Most organizations and people within them have a set of rules by which they play the game of business. Some common rules for doing business are:

- Companies run from the top down in a hierarchy
- Employees need offices from which to work
- Strategic planning is a once-a-year event
- Customers must be happy with what your company makes

Rules exist within a corporation for very good reasons. Most often they are built on past habits of success with the intention of assuring future success. Complete a past process correctly and receive the same successful result. This is true as long as the environment in which that process operates doesn't change. As soon as environmental change enters into the equation, past habits of success do not guarantee future successful results.

Often rules become institutionalized. New employees with MBAs come into the work force with a well-developed sense of rules. These rules are based on past successes that have been memorialized as case studies. As long as the environment in which that case study was successful remains the same, it is reasonable to expect similar results based on an ability to execute the rule correctly.

Rules are very difficult to break for most people in a company, because they do not have the *authority* to break them, even if they have been given the *responsibility* to do it. Part of the reason for the difficulty is that people do not see better or more effective ways to do things.

As the environment changes, however, pressure is increasingly applied to companies to discover new ways of playing the game. Companies that are most likely to win the game are ones that are focused on satisfying their customer's customer.

Know How to Help Your *Customers Help* Their *Customers*

For you to create an effective relationship requires fundamental shifts in understanding, from just focusing on your customer to now focusing on your customer's customer. That means **you must understand how your product or service solution is going to help your customer help their customer.**

For example, let's take the rule that says decision-making is a hierarchical top-down process. In a manufacturing environment, this means that market estimates are done so that predictions can be made to determine what needs to be produced to meet customer needs. These market estimates are based on interviews with current customers and statistical projections based on past sales volume.

Many forward-thinking companies have changed this. They now provide information systems that the manufacturing company's customer taps into to place orders directly. Now that company has day-to-day sales data, which enables it to have more accurate production estimates. And with software that focuses on "Supply Chain Management," all of the customers who incorporate a product into their product have a chance to influence what gets produced.

Know the Color of Your Customer's Lenses

The largest challenge you face as a sales professional is understanding the perceptual filters your prospect is wearing. Often your prospect asks for ideas that allow them to enhance or streamline what is already being done. If you are proposing something more radical to a lower-level person, you will run into perceptual roadblocks. Higher-level people in the organization are often more concerned with more innovative ways to do things. But, even this is not a rule.

The following is an interesting viewpoint written by Thornton May in an issue of *Imaging World:*

> The majority of proposed information-systems solutions were turned down by chief financial officers because the proposals failed to generate an adequate return on investment. They concurred that the proposals were not revolutionary enough.

> *The rejected proposals would simply have streamlined existing processes, producing small financial returns. If the applications had redesigned those processes to achieve not only cost reduction but also revenue enhancement, they would have received the CFO's approval.*

Your situation analysis of a prospect needs to take into consideration that company's operating environment. You need to know how they operate, who their customers are, who their competition is, and how their marketplace is changing. If you do this before you meet with the prospect, you will have a much better chance of discovering that person's perceptual filters and how difficult or easy it's going to be to make a sale. To understand the perceptions of your customer, you not only need to "walk a mile in their shoes," you must also know which road they are on.

Interphase: Opening the Relationship
Step 1: Research

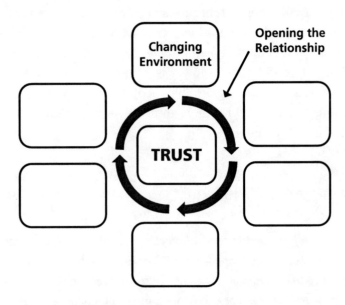

Let's envision working with a new prospect. You've been cold-calling the company for some time and your efforts have finally resulted in an appointment. You want to make a good impression and use the PeopleSavvy skills you've learned to create a long-term, profitable relationship.

Before your meeting, do your homework. Read the company website. Specifically, you are gaining an understanding of who they are, what they do, and who their customers are. Next, do some additional homework on the company. You can Google the company and uncover lots of information about the company and what their customers think about the company. Check out Hoovers, an online reference, to see what their financials look like and who their competitors are. If the person you're meeting with is a corporate officer, you might even find their bio in Hoovers.

Look for Connections

Next, do some in-depth investigation of the individual you are meeting with. On some company websites you can enter search criteria, so if there is a press release about the person or something the person said you can access that information. Go to Google and enter the person's name with quotes around the name. You may find additional information about the person—membership in industry trade groups, non-profit groups, etc. Check out classmates.com to see if the person might be listed there.

> I was meeting with the CEO of a company. In addition to the great information about him through Google, I found that he had a listing on classmates.com and had completed a survey on his lifestyle. I now knew the name of his spouse and the names of his three children. I also knew the city where he lived and what kind of car he drove. Knowing the city where he lived allowed me to check

> *online phone directories to get an exact address and home phone number.*
>
> *Having his high school information and graduation date allowed me to search online with the local newspaper's archives, where I gathered additional facts about what was going on when he was growing up. I found out that he was a star on the school's baseball team.*
>
> *So, knowing where he lived and the kind of car he drove told me a lot about his values and lifestyle, which are tied into primary motivators. Knowing that he grew up playing sports and was good at it gave me insights into how he likely viewed and chose to work in the world. It may also be an indication of his negotiation style.*
>
> *Having gained it, did I share all of this information when I met him? No!*

The only reason to collect this information is to find areas of commonality to connect with the person. What have you done in your life that is similar to what they have done? Having this information gives you the ability to broach topics of discussion that allow the relationship to grow naturally and comfortably. Do not mention that you know where they live or have information about their family. Rather than creating a sense of connection, that can foster suspicion or distrust.

Continually Collect Data...

Over time, as you deepen the relationship, a customer may mention additional personal information to you. Often they will not remember that they have done that. For example, you may have an appointment scheduled that they have to cancel because their son, Jeff, has to be picked up from school. If you didn't have the son's name before, you now have it. However, most people will not remember comments that are made in passing, so don't assume that you can bring up their son's name in conversation.

...And Assure You Can Access It

What do you do with all of this data that you're collecting? Just log it into your electronic profile on the individual. It is all raw data, some of which is likely to pay off down the line in building your relationship. However, for the time being, you are just collecting it.

Remember, though, that collecting data is only useful if you can later *access* it. Your company may be using ACT or Goldmine or an online database such as Salesforce.com to make this practical. Creating a system where you can store and easily access this data is critical to your long-term success. The need for these systems increases exponentially as the number of clients you service grows.

Interphase: Opening the Relationship
Step 2: Meeting Preparation

As you think through the Trust Model and how to use it for your first meeting, your initial objective should be to listen compassion-ately. If you've done your homework, you know enough about the company and what their issues are that you can ask intelligent questions that come up in a natural way in this first conversation.

If you focus your preparation on polishing your "pitch" for the first meeting, you'll be viewed as "just another vendor." If you use the same information to develop a list of questions that allow you to probe deeper into possible issues and areas of concern, you'll be viewed as a potential strategic business partner.

Asking questions will allow you to progress from rapport to trust, because the questions will cause the prospect to start viewing you as competent and possibly committed to her desired-end-results.

As you prepare your questions, think about what kind of answers you might get to the questions. Then start thinking about the questions you'll ask if you get specific answers. In this way, you can script out a complete sales call prior to the meeting. You'll be more relaxed on the call because you'll be focused on listening to the prospect instead of worrying about what you'll say next—or worse, not focusing on the deeper issues and presenting (wrong) solutions too soon. If you've anticipated her answers to your questions, you'll have your next question ready to ask.

In other words, asking the right questions and anticipating the response so you can ask the next good question will allow you to guide the conversation productively and demonstrate to the prospect that you are, indeed, a competent business partner.

Compassionate listening is the critical skill for building rapport with your clients. It also allows them to see that you are different; you're not immediately telling them why you and your company are the best thing since Velcro.

Interphase: Opening the Relationship

Step 3: First Meeting

Let's suppose that your first meeting takes place in the prospect's office. As you walk in, make eye contact and acknowledge this very important person in front of you. It's OK to glance around the office and at her desk to see what's there. You may notice certain books in her bookcase, pictures on the wall, etc. Just make a mental note at this point. If there's something on the wall or on her desk that ties in to the reason for your meeting, it's appropriate to discuss it during the first meeting.

Having said that, I tend not to comment about anything in the prospect's office during the first meeting. I'm there to gain an understanding of issues and possible solutions I can offer the person. I'm also very focused on building a good level of rapport and move as quickly as possible to trust. Observation comments may or may not move me toward that objective.

In the chitchat phase of the meeting, which usually lasts from 10 seconds to several minutes, I will notice several things:

- Quickness or slowness of speech – voice tempo
- Pitch of their voice – voice tone
- Loudness of their voice – voice volume
- Depth and speed of breathing – breathing patterns
- Preferences in the way they sit or stand – body postures

I choose one or two things to **mirror.** It might be her voice tone and tempo. It might be the way she holds her hands when she talks. It could be something totally unconscious for most people, like her breathing patterns. The objective here is to create a physiological connection as part of the rapport-building process.

I'll also notice whether the person seems to be outgoing or reserved and if they talk about what they do or the people they work with. Those two items will give me a very good idea about the person's **behavioral style.**

If you've done your homework, you will ask your questions and give the prospect a sense that you are competent and committed to her desired-end-results. I highly recommend taking notes during this part of the call. **You can copy down exact phrases she uses when responding to your questions (this will be very valuable when you do your presentation).** The prospect will generally appreciate someone who is taking notes, as most people believe that what they are saying is important and your taking notes indicates to them that you recognize this importance.

You may be given the opportunity to make an immediate presentation or be asked to schedule another meeting to make a presentation. I almost always opt for a second meeting. I usually tell the prospect that she has given me a lot to think about (she has!) and I need some time to digest her communication. I say that I would like to come back with a well-thought-out approach to her needs, rather than just do a feature-and-benefit dump. (Keep in mind, though, that your company's sales approach may be different and this should be discussed with your sales manager.)

When the meeting ends, go out to your car or find a quiet place and start downloading everything you noticed about the prospect's office and the meeting. Ask yourself the following eight key questions and add the answers to the notes you've already taken.

1. What was on her walls?
2. What was on her desk?
3. What seemed most important to her?
4. Did she react, either positively or negatively, to certain questions?
5. What do you think her behavioral style and communication styles are?
6. Were there other people present in the meeting?
7. Who were they and what were their names?
8. Did she mention other people that might be involved in the sale?

Downloading these notes while they are still fresh is critical to your success with the prospect.

All of this information will be used to construct a presentation that ties in specifically with her stated needs and with her motivators, behavioral style, and communication style. Your ability to notice and document these things is critical to the presentation you'll be crafting.

Phase 2: Recognizing Needs
or
Knowing the Right Questions, Asking the Right Person

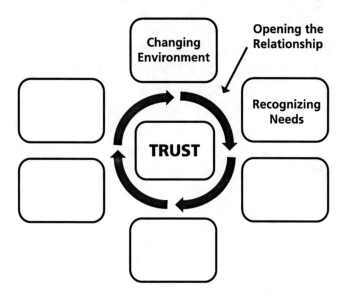

For your prospect, this phase usually begins with a perceptual awareness that the current environment has changed to a degree requiring some action. Should your prospect come face-to-face with a competitor's advantage, for instance, this creates the perception of new needs.

For example, in many companies the time-value of information provides the competitive advantage. If I know market conditions and my financial status before you know the same about your company, I can beat you to market with products or programs that allow me to be viewed as innovative. You may reach the same conclusion I do, but if you follow me to market, your customers may view your effort as copying my innovations.

The recognition of needs comes from dissatisfaction with the current situation. Recognizing that *something* needs to be changed does not mean that the prospect is going to know exactly *what* needs to be changed.

So, what do customers want or need? At a higher executive level, they want competitive advantage that either helps them make money or save money. At lower levels, they need the products and services that enable these competitive advantages to come to fruition.

For example, one of your prospects has discussed a need. From a top-down need analysis we might ask the following questions of a senior executive.

- What is the benefit to your company?
- How are you trying to enhance relationships with your customers?
- What is the benefit to your customer's business?
- If you implement this strategy what, specifically, will change—shrinking inventory, improving profits, cutting receivables, or reducing response times?

Speaking with a lower-level buyer, they might not know the answers to the above questions. So we may be required to ask lower-level questions.

- Which type of product or service do you need to meet your customer's specifications?
- What are your branch offices going to use?
- Who needs to be involved in this decision process?

Depending on your product or service, you may be selling to the senior-level executive or to a lower-level buyer. The funny thing is, it doesn't really matter, because your product or service will ultimately impact the competitive advantage of the prospect's company. However, **your ability to position or differentiate your product or service based on competitive advantage—as perceived by the person you are dealing with—in fact positions you as either a business partner or just another vendor who may happen to have the lowest price.** The prospect's perception of your ability to deliver competitive advantage takes place at this stage of the buying process, not during product or service evaluation. It is here that you will uncover the perceptual rules that allow you to frame your solution or reframe any objections that might come up.

Phase 3: Assessing Options
or
Putting Your Best Face Forward

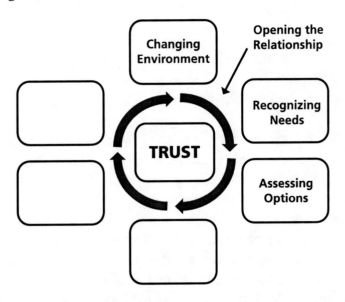

A critical misunderstanding on the part of salespeople happens at this stage in the buying process. Many salespeople are very happy when they receive a request for proposal/quote (RFP/RFQ). The good news is you have just been invited to the dance. The bad news is you have no idea what kind of tune you'll be expected to dance to (i.e., you don't know what the prospect's decision-making criteria are). Worse, you have not had an opportunity to influence those criteria or perceptions of needs. Your competitors may have already done this. If you've been involved with a significant number of RFP/RFQs, you have probably seen an RFP/RFQ that looks like it was tailor-made for one of your competitors.

Differentiating Yourself from the Competition

Your job at this stage is to differentiate your product or service from those of your competitors. To effectively do this, you use all of the psychological data you uncovered in the "recognizing needs" stage.

Not knowing this information, you may be at a loss as to how to differentiate yourself from competitors or how to emphasize those things that will have greatest impact on the prospect.

You differentiate yourself from your competitors by providing value. You create value by helping your customer become more competitive.

Value judgments are made based on perceptions. These perceptions include such things as the reputation of your company, advertising, professionalism, your appearance, or information provided in the sales presentation. They also include the prospect's own motivations, behavioral style, and communication style. You need to be able to meet and influence all of your buyer's perceptions.

No matter how well you explain the features, advantages, and benefits of your solution, your prospect cannot always accurately understand how you might lower their costs or raise their performance. Your prospects will not pay for solutions they can't perceive. You may be offering hard, quantifiable value, but it may be rejected by the prospect. Why? Because, you have not **framed** the information in a way that the prospect can understand from a deep motivational level.

It is critical that you understand how to deal with the emotions and feelings of your prospects. This may be a challenge for you, basically, if you are used to dealing with "hard facts" such as financial data.

Getting to the Real Buyer

Individual decision-makers purchase value, not products and services. Both *perceived* value and *quantifiable* value are assessed and examined by the decision-maker. Who the decision-maker is influences the value attributed to the product or service. In other words, **lower-level buyers will perceive value based more on features and benefits. Higher-level buyers will perceive value based more on gaining competitive advantages.**

Clearly identifying the value you create for a prospect and their perceptions of value rests on your ability to accurately identify the actual decision-maker. The expertise and sources of information you provide the decision-maker will shape what perceptions will persuade them. PeopleSavvy will assist you in knowing what to say to the decision-maker. However, it is not focused on determining the real buyer, because in many, possibly most cases you will know who the decision-maker is. If you would like an excellent and detailed approach to this, read *Strategic Selling* by Robert Miller and Stephen Heiman.

Demonstrating Lowering Total Cost of Operation

Even when your product or service has a higher sticker price than your competitors', by **reframing** you may be able to demonstrate how, in the long run, it lowers total cost of operation. This is another example of enlarging the frame.

For a simple example of lowering total cost of operation, consider the selling of a computer printer. Your printer is more expensive than a competitor's model. Your prospect may make a decision only on acquisition cost. Unless you take the time to point out that the prospect has a network and your printer includes built-in network capability (an expensive add-on for the competitor), consumable costs are lower and duty cycle life is higher. Pointing out these features is only the first step; you must ensure that the prospect associates some value to these features—saving money over the life of the printer, for example.

Less obvious examples of lowering total cost of operation are a function of how the business operates. Taking our printer example again, if the printer is used in a workgroup you might save interest expense on capital expenditures for new equipment because you only bought one printer for the workgroup instead of multiple printers.

Let's take it a step further. Assume that this printer is connected to a client/server network with remote printing capabilities. Now an executive could print out something for the workgroup and not have to hand-carry the document to that group. Depending on how far the executive's office was from the workgroup, we could factor in further cost savings.

Taking it to extremes, let's assume that the printer has now lived out its useful accounting depreciable life. Your competitor's product has long since died, but yours is still functional. Your customer's company has just created an EDI system with its customers, supplying them with used but functional computers so they can log on directly to your customer's system. Your printer now enters a second life cycle, allowing your customer to provide value to one of its customers with little associated cost.

If you are going to create value for your customer, you must do this downstream cost analysis, regardless of what your product or service is. Even if you have the least expensive product or service on the market, a sharp competitor could still beat you by providing downstream costs that significantly impact the perceptions of the prospect.

The greater the acquisition cost of the product or service you are selling, the more you need to tie that cost in to saving money by impacting business processes. Remember that savings from purchases or operations drop right to the bottom line and significantly impact the profitability of the prospect's company.

Some other ways you can lower your buyer's costs:

- Lower delivery, installation, or financing cost
- Lower direct cost of using the product (i.e., requires less maintenance, less space, or less energy)
- Lower risk of failure

If you are going to differentiate your offering based on cost, you must chart in detail how your product impacts the prospect's business processes. That means you know every use, current and/or planned, and have associated an impact cost for the effective life of the product.

Raising Buyer Performance

If cost isn't the issue, another way you can support greater perceived value is by raising buyer performance. Raising buyer performance for the prospect's company involves:

- raising their level of satisfaction,
- meeting needs, or
- creating prestige for the company.

Prestige is just as important as the features, advantages, or benefits of the product or service you are offering.

Prestige is a value perception that originates from within the buyer or the person who established the corporate culture (who may be long dead, but still influences how the company operates). **Raising buyer performance depends on understanding what is desirable performance from the prospect's point of view, not**

from your point of view. Raising the performance of the prospect depends on what creates differentiation with their customers. Each company ultimately wants a competitive advantage that allows it to differentiate itself from its competitors in the minds of its customers.

As long as you meet or exceed the value expectations of your prospects, you create satisfied customers and can count on repeat business. If your prospects sense a gap between your offering and their expectations of value, they may suddenly become unhappy or choose a different vendor.

To build effective relationships, you need to know the prospect better than they know themselves. This means you must have enough information about your prospect to make recommendations that fit their needs and really solve key issues. Understand what it is that makes them so pleased with your product or service that your competitor's discount won't be of interest. Knowing their **primary motivators and behavioral styles** will take you a long way down that road.

Making the Presentation

Regardless of the focus of your presentation—for example, "lowering total cost of ownership"—you need to make a presentation that is persuasive.

If you've taken significant notes from your meeting(s), the prospect has supplied all of the information to exactly sell them. By now you've got exact **emotional word pictures** they use. You know their **voice tone and tempo,** their **behavioral style** and **primary motivators.**

You'll need to construct a presentation that includes all of these elements. Essentially, you are telling the prospect how your solution meets their exact needs. You're using the same emotional word pictures they used to communicate with you. You're tying in their primary motivators and making a presentation appropriate for their behavioral style.

For example, your customer has *recognition* as his primary motivator; he is a *high "D"* behavioral style and primarily *visual* communication style. Knowing this, you can tailor your presentation to talk directly to him in a language he understands from all levels.

- With recognition as his motivator, you know your presentation will need to communicate how he will be recognized by his company for making a buying decision that has created competitive advantage.
- As he is a high "D," you'll need to make your presentation short and sweet. Spending a lot of time on the minutia will result in his getting bored and your possibly losing the sale.
- Since he perceives the world visually, you'll want to have visuals in your presentation; they don't have to be very detailed, just something that a high "D" can glance at. If you have a handout as part of your presentation, make sure it has a well-written executive summary, as that will be the only part a high "D" will personally read. The balance of the handout may be given to lower-level people to scrutinize.

If your customer has *money*, specifically saving money, as her primary motivator and she is a *high "C"* with an *auditory* communication style, you would make a very different presentation.

- In this case, you would focus on lowering the total cost of ownership and
- take a significant amount of time discussing all of the details of your solution.
- This presentation would be more of a dialogue between the two of you. If you delivered a PowerPoint-based stand-up presentation, she might lose interest. Since she's a high "C" with an extensive need for details, your PowerPoint would need to be very comprehensive.

These are examples of two very different people requiring two very different presentations. Your ability to accurately assess the customer's psychological makeup is critical to ensuring that you make the correct presentation.

While these resources can really help you customize your presentation to communicate to the needs of the customer, what if you're presenting to a group and there are various makeups represented? The answer is quite logical: Tailor your presentation to the ultimate decision-maker.

If you think the decision will be made by consensus, you may need to be flexible. You do this by developing your presentation three or four different ways (to accommodate the specifics of each person). When you speak to each individual, you would subtly change your language and behavior based on that individual's needs. This can get rather complex and requires significant practice to accomplish seamlessly.

Phase 4: Resolving Concerns
or
Dealing with the Details

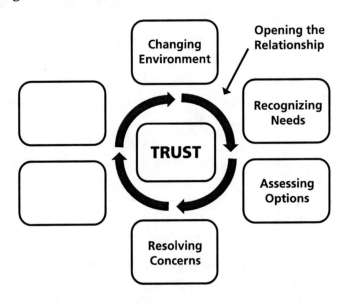

You're in the final running. The prospect has narrowed the selection to one or two finalists. This is where "resolving concerns" takes place. Even if you're the first choice, you do not have the sale locked up.

Trust is the largest motivator at this point in the process. Yet if you try to establish trust now, you will fail because your efforts will appear to be insincere. Trust-building, the very foundation of relationship-selling, needs to start at the very beginning and be reinforced throughout the process. This is because salespeople, as a stereotype, are often perceived as being willing to say or do anything to get the sale.

A number of years ago, Isuzu Motors had a commercial on television that featured Joe Isuzu. Joe would make outlandish claims about the car. With a totally straight face and sincere look in his eye, he would say things like, "It has more seats than the Superdome!" At the end of his pitch he'd give a phony smile and say, "You can trust me."

These ads were obviously a spoof on car salesmen. By taking it to an extreme, the company was implying they knew the games car salesmen play and by exposing them, it would be apparent they would not resort to them.

Unfortunately, unless you consistently demonstrate to your customer that you are trustworthy, you may be lumped into the Joe Isuzu category.

Lack of trust leads to fear. When your prospect begins to experience doubts or fear, they may ask themselves, "What if this all goes wrong?" It's not really so much the fear of something going wrong; it's more the fear of what's going to happen to *them* if this goes wrong.

It is in the *resolving concerns* phase that the classic sales process begins to fall apart. It is usually at this point that most salespeople begin to apply standard "closing" techniques to push the customer past their indecision. Yet imagine for a moment that you are making a major purchase and the salesperson across from you begins to hardball-close you. What would be your natural response? Most likely you would begin to think of reasons why you should slow down the sales process. You'd begin to object to certain terms and conditions. Who created the objections? The salesperson did.

So, what concerns and issues do prospects have to resolve in the face of change? Knowing them will assist you in maintaining and building on the trust you have established in the earlier phases.

- Fear of loss of control: Change requires people to go from being on top of things to being unsure and feeling out of control. They go through a learning phase, during which they need extra handholding.
- Fear of uncertainty: The future is not obvious and they may feel as if they are about to walk off a cliff. Some prospects may want to see all the details of the plan and want to examine all contingencies. Knowing a person's **behavioral style** will help you with the steps you need to take with this kind of person.
- Fear of surprises: Keeping the prospect up to date is critical. Last-minute changes with little advance warning are unacceptable.
- Concerns generated by habits: We all have habits. Habits are efficient, effective, and allow us to be mindless. Changing to new ways of doing things is uncomfortable and often requires additional mental effort. In other words, change requires us to be mindful instead of mindless.
- Belief that new processes mean more work (which may be correct): Preparing the prospect for new methods and more work is absolutely necessary.
- Concern for competence: People often question their ability to master new processes, particularly if training and ongoing support is not provided or are viewed with skepticism.
- Lack of skills: New ways require people to learn skills that they may not have. These are sometimes perceived as being difficult to acquire.
- Time to adjust: Saying "do it differently" is not enough. It takes time for new skills and a sense of comfort to develop. Rushing leads to disruptions, sabotage, resistance, and poor performance.

In the chapter on trust, you learned that you communicate your competence and commitment to the customer's desired-end-result based on what you *ask,* not on what you *tell,* the person. When your customer starts to get nervous is the time for you to demonstrate your compassion and ask detailed questions about the concerns they have. By helping the customer develop an understanding of the issues that are coming forward, you'll be viewed differently from the salesperson who, at this point, starts using aggressive closing techniques.

If you've been in sales for a while, it is likely that you have heard the same objections to your product or service several times. Some of these objections may be because of certain ways your company does business. Some of them may be planted by your competitors. I recommended earlier that you take all of the objections that you hear and start to develop multiple responses to them. What specifically is the objection? What is the implication or consequence of that objection to the client? Are there any **implied rules** in that objection?

Let's say your company is very small, so the rule might be that your company can't handle a large order. After cataloging all of the objections, start to craft responses. Think about how you might **reframe** a person's perception—as Ronald Reagan did in the example in the communication chapter. If the objection is inaccurate, how might you present information to clarify the truth? Be very careful about giving rebuttals, as people will often look at your response wondering if you are hiding something or only being defensive.

If your customer brings up your competition, you can discuss how it's good to have competition because it makes everyone better. **When you discuss your competition, use language that is not your customer's preferred style.** For example, if your customer is an auditory, use visual words when describing the competitor.

Even though you are being complimentary to your competitor, your customer will have to work hard translating your words into their preferred mode. That need to "work hard" to understand will be attributed to the competition, not you.

Phase 5: Promise Acceptance
or
Gaining—and Keeping—the Sale

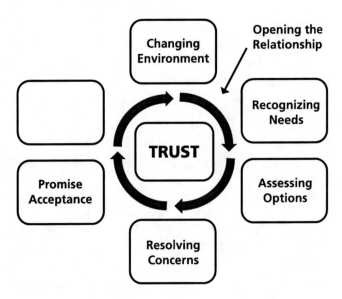

If the results of your negotiations are positive, you move to the next stage—signing some sort of contract that indicates your customer's commitment to proceed with the purchase. In a home sale, often a very deep breath from the customer accompanies this stage, because buying a home is often the largest single purchase a person will make in their lifetime. For many people, the feelings that accompany this event are like stepping off the edge of a cliff.

What you are selling may not elicit such strong feelings from your customer, but they are making a commitment to purchase—and there is some perceived risk in this. So there is almost always some final question as to the real need of what is being purchased.

It's painful to watch a young salesperson who has the sale sewn up, continue selling and ultimately lose the sale. If you were helping a close friend make a purchase, how would you act? What would you say? It's possible that you would provide quiet assurance to your friend that they, in fact, are making the correct decision. Or you might choose to be silent at this point, as the decision is really your friend's, not yours.

One of the most effective strategies top-producing sales professionals use is to create a vacuum. They literally pull back from the table and create a void of silence.

One sales professional I know was in the final stages of leasing a huge block of office space to a Fortune 100 company. The commission he would receive was in the hundreds of thousands of dollars.

When he delivered the lease documents to the vice president who was to sign the lease, he put the documents on the desk and sat down in a chair to the side and didn't say a word. For thirty minutes. The vice president just looked at the documents during this time.

Finally the VP picked up a pen, signed the documents, and pushed them across his desk toward the salesperson.

As the salesperson was putting the documents in his briefcase, the vice president told him that if he had said one word, he would not have signed and would have re-opened negotiations.

If your customer chooses to ask questions or make requests at this point, write them down. These are the final promises that you make and it is here that the **depth of trust** will be measured. If you casually say, "Of course we can get that for you," you have just made a promise. You had better remember it and make sure it is carried out.

If you recall, the final step in the **Trust Model** is *consistency.* If you promise something and then don't deliver on your promise, you'll be viewed as inconsistent. That will set a very shallow level of trust in the mind of the customer, and **once you set a shallow level of trust, you won't be able to deepen it, no matter how hard your work at it.** Essentially, there will always be a nagging doubt on the part of the customer: "Will he really deliver on this promise?"

To avoid risking this, make sure you continue asking questions of your customer. If they want you to make a promise, you need to understand in great detail what "promise fulfillment" looks, sounds, and feels like to the client. If you don't know those exact expectations, you'll not likely meet them.

Phase 6: Promise Delivery
or
Keeping Your Word and Deepening Trust

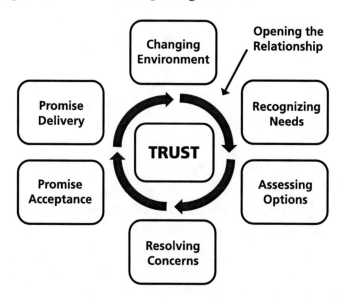

Fulfillment of promise is where the rubber meets the road in all relationships. Your ability as a sales professional to shape the expectations of promise for your buyer is critical to establishing a long-term relationship. "Under promise and over deliver" may be an old adage; however, it's a good guideline and a big key to successful business relationships.

You may be involved in installation, after-sales support, and continuing contact with the prospect. **The period after the decision is a very fertile area of sales opportunity.** You need to either track what gets delivered to the customer or hand off your promise sheet to the people in your company who will have responsibility to deliver the promise. Then make sure they follow through.

If the customer comes away from the business transaction feeling like what was promised wasn't delivered, they will blame the salesperson. And rightfully so. Customers have an expectation that you won't sell them something you can't deliver. And, yet, salespeople are always pushing the edge of the envelope to ensure that they meet or exceed their sales quota. It's a tricky balance, but one that sales professionals have mastered.

Your key strategy is to *over-communicate*. That means that you communicate with your customer and you communicate with the various departments inside your own organization, etc. Communicating means taking the time to ensure that everyone is not only on the same page, but reading the same book.

Despite the many resistances to change, you have a variety of methods available to ease the transition.

- Involve the customer as much as you can in the change-planning process. Participation leads to ownership and enthusiasm.
- Communicate clearly, and often, what you are trying to achieve. Provide the firm's staff with as much detail as you can.
- Divide the implementation of change into manageable, comprehensible stages. Make the stages as familiar as possible. Keep the first stages small and easy, and make sure they are guaranteed successes.
- Allow no surprises; communicate constantly.
- Let commitment grow. Do not ask for a pledge of allegiance to new, untried ways.
- Make clear what will be expected of people after the change. Carefully and fully communicate standards and requirements.

Interphase: Extending the Relationship
or
Preparing for the Next Sale...and the Next

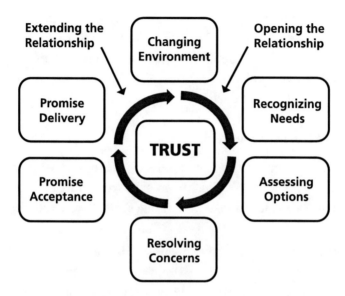

If you truly want to demonstrate commitment to the customer and short-circuit your competition by limiting their participation in the customer's buying process, you need to help the customer anticipate the future.

At this point in the buying process, you've developed a great deal of understanding about the customer and their business processes, customers, and culture. If you supply information and ideas that help them get a clearer perspective on what might happen in the next six months or even the next six years, they will view you as a "strategic business partner," not just another salesperson.

For example, when you read an article that might have some consequences for your customer's business, clip the article and send it to them. They may have already seen it, so attach a note saying, "You've probably already seen this, but just in case you haven't…" At a minimum, they will appreciate that you are still considering their future.

Even if your company has a customer service department, make a regular part of your sales efforts to follow up with your customer and find out how it's going. They will continue to remember you, they might have a referral for you, or you may get an opportunity to meet your previous customer's replacement.

Now Roll Up Your Sleeves

Though this is unquestionably a book on increasing your sales and income, essentially you've just been exposed to three semesters of psychology. It's a lot to take in and digest. Is it worth it? Yes!!!

Many of my clients who have been working on this for more than 10 years are now the top professionals in their company—and in many cases, their industry. Some of these professionals have doubled or even tripled their sales revenue over a three-year period after gaining facility with applying the very skills I have revealed to you. I am talking here about men and women who in some cases were struggling or just starting up, and in other cases were already doing extremely well.

In all cases, their lifestyles have changed immeasurably for the better. And what do they consistently tell me? That many of their customers have also become good friends who provide them with a constant stream of referrals.

Have they stopped cold-calling? In the literal sense of the word, yes. These professionals now look at it as warm-calling. They have a mindset that the next person they meet in a business setting might just be their new best friend, as well as a valuable customer who continues to enhance their lifestyle.

Can what happened to them happen to you? Absolutely. Will it? That's up to you. Reading the book will help you gain understanding. However, it's the practicing of these techniques that will give you the experience. And that will make the difference.

Are you willing to put forth the effort and venture into new behavioral territory? Are you willing to be patient with yourself as you sharpen new skills? Are you prepared to practice new behaviors on your friends and family and maybe look or sound a little foolish from time to time? That's what it takes to gain ability with any new information or skill. But the rewards...well, you can imagine what they can be.

Are you ready to see major improvement in your sales results? You hold the keys to your greater success right in your hands. It all has to do with your *PeopleSavvy.*

OKAY, I'VE READ THE BOOK. NOW WHAT?

If PeopleSavvy makes sense to you, there are a number of things you can do to expand your repertoire of resources and make these skills more easily and naturally accessible to you.

• Accept Our Free Gift

While this is our shameless approach to getting you on our contact list (though we promise not to bother you unless you actually opt-in), you will find plenty of value in our Special Report: The Next Best Thing to Mind Reading. Consider it a bonus chapter for the PeopleSavvy for Sales Professionals book.

In this report you will learn scientifically based keys—cues not based on body language—for effectively and reliably "reading" your prospect and knowing how they are thinking in any and every situation.

To receive this information-rich report go to www.peoplesavvy.com/eyes.htm, fill out the contact box, and enter **Chapter-6** in the box labeled "key."

• Take a PeopleSavvy 1- or 2-Day Seminar

Do you really want to anchor your PeopleSavvy skills in the bedrock of experience? There is literally no better way to enhance your effectiveness than participating in a PeopleSavvy seminar. See the skills demonstrated, practice them yourself, and get straight on answers to your specific questions.

To learn where and when the next public PeopleSavvy seminar will be held, go to www.peoplesavvy.com, click on PeopleSavvy and select "Public Seminar," or contact us directly about an in-house session for your people.

• Get a Detailed Behavioral Profile

You can be most effective using your PeopleSavvy skills if you know your own behavioral profile. We are pleased to provide a detailed 20+ page report complete with analysis of your behavioral style, insights into your motivational factors, strategies for increasing effectiveness, and more.

To get the full story or to order your personal Behavioral Profile, go to www.savvybooks.com/profile.htm.

ABOUT PEOPLESAVVY SEMINARS

In addition to those open to the public, customized seminars based on PeopleSavvy key principles are available to business, educational, and community groups throughout the United States and Canada. They include:

PeopleSavvy for Sales Professionals
PeopleSavvy for Leaders
PeopleSavvy for Managers
PeopleSavvy for Non-Profits

For more information, visit:
www.peoplesavvy.com

or contact:

Stebbins Consulting Group
944 Princeton Drive
Marina del Rey, CA 90292
310-578-5322

Dr. Stebbins is also available for speaking engagements.
310-578-5322 or sales@peoplesavvy.com

BIBLIOGRAPHY

Abbeduto, Leonard; Laurie Furman, and Betty Davies. Identifying speech acts
from contextual and linguistic information. *Language and Speech* Vol.
32(3) (July-September 1989): 189-203.

Abratt, R. Industrial buying in high-tech markets. *Industrial Marketing
Management* Vol. 15 (1986): 293-8.

Acheson, Kerri L. "The effects of psychological type and interpersonal psychological distance on selling effectiveness in a service industry." PhD
diss., *Dissertation Abstracts International* 50(7-A) (January 1990): 21-33.

Ahearne, Michael, C. B. Bhattacharya, and Thomas Gruen. Antecedents and
Consequences of Customer-Company Identification: Expanding the Role
of Relationship Marketing. *Journal of Applied Psychology* 90(3), (May
2005): 574-585.

Ahearne, Michael, John Mathieu, and Adam Rapp. To Empower or Not to Empower
Your Sales Force? An Empirical Examination of the Influence of Leadership
Empowerment Behavior on Customer Satisfaction and Performance.
Journal of Applied Psychology 90(5) (September 2005): 945-955.

Ailes, Roger. *You Are The Message.* Homewood, IL: Dow Jones-Irwin;
Doubleday, 1987.

Alessandra, Anthony, and Phil Wexler. Breaking tradition: The sales pitch as
customer service. *Training and Development Journal* Vol 39(11)
(November 1985): 41-43.

Alessandra, Tony, Phil Wexler, and Rick Barrera. *Non- Manipulative Selling.*
Saddle River, NJ: Prentice Hall, 1987.

Allport, G.W., and P.E. Vernon. *The Study of Values.* Boston: Houghton Mifflin, 1931.

Anderson, Craig A. Motivational and performance deficits in interpersonal
settings: The effect of attributional style. *Journal of Personality and
Social Psychology* Vol 45(5) (November 1983): 1136-1147.

Anderson, Erin, Wujin Chu, and Barton Weitz. Industrial purchasing: An empirical exploration of the buyclass framework. *Journal of Marketing* Vol
51(3) (July 1987): 71-86.

Anderson, Erin, and Richard L. Oliver. Perspectives on behavior-based versus
outcome-based salesforce control systems. *Journal of Marketing* Vol
51(4) (October 1987): 76-88.

Andrews, Patricia H. Gender differences in persuasive communication and attribution of success and failure. *Human Communication Research* Vol 13(3) (Spring 1987): 372-385.

Armbruster, Wally. *Where Have All The Salesmen Gone?* St. Louis, MO: Piraeus Press, 1982.

Assmus, Gert, John U. Farley, and Donald R. Lehmann. How advertising affects sales: Meta-analysis of econometric results. *Journal of Marketing Research* Vol 21(1) (February 1984): 65-74.

Axsom, Danny, Suzanne Yates, and Shelley Chaiken. Audience response as a heuristic cue in persuasion. *Journal of Personality and Social Psychology* Vol 53(1) (July 1987): 30-40.

Baglan, Thomas, James Lalumia, and Ovid L. Bayless. Utilization of compliance-gaining strategies: A research note. *Communication Monographs* Vol 53(3) (September 1986): 289-293.

Bagozzi, R. P. Salesforce performance and satisfaction as a function of individual difference, interpersonal, and situational factors. *Journal of Marketing Research* no.15 (1978): 517-531.

Bandler, Richard, and John Grinder. *Reframing.* Moab, UT: Real People Press, 1982.

Bannister, D., and J.M.M. Mair. *The Evaluation of Personal Constructs.* London: Academic Press, 1968.

Bankart, C. Peter, and Ralph L. Olson. Internally and socially based determinants of the acceptance of persuasive communications. *Journal of Social Psychology* Vol 126(6) (December 1986): 715-724.

Barclay, D. W. Interdepartmental conflict in organizational buying: the impact of the organizational context. *Journal of Marketing Research* Vol. 28 (1991): 145-59.

Bateson, Gregory. Steps *To An Ecology of Mind.* Canada: Chandler Publishing, 1972.

Batten, Bruce W., and Chester A. Insko. Detection of speaker's attitude from successive pro and con advocacy. *Representative Research in Social Psychology* Vol 16(2) (1986): 28-37.

Baumgardner, Michael H., Michael R. Leippe, David L. Ronis, and Anthony G. Greenwald. In search of reliable persuasion effects: II. Associative interference and persistence of persuasion in a message-dense environment. *Journal of Personality and Social Psychology* Vol 45(3) (September 1983): 524-537.

Beaman, Arthur L., Nancy M. Steblay, Marilyn Preston, and Bonnel Klentz. Compliance as a function of elapsed time between first and second requests. *Journal of Social Psychology* Vol 128(2) (April 1988): 233-243.

Beatty, Sharon E. An exploratory study of organizational values with a focus on people orientation. *Journal of Retailing* Vol 64(4) (Winter 1988): 405-425.

Beck, Kenneth H., and Clive M. Davis. The effects of false physiological feedback and subject relevance upon belief acceptance. *Social Behavior and Personality* Vol 10(2) (1982): 213-220.

Becker, B. W., and P.E. Connor. Personal values of the heavy user of mass media. *Journal of Advertising Research* 21 (1981): 37-43.

Becker, B. W. and P.E. Connor. "The Influence of Personal Values on Attitude and Store Choice Behavior." In *An Assessment of Marketing Thought and Practice,* edited by B. J. Walker, W. O. Bearden, W. R. Darden, P. E. Murphy, J. R. Nevin, J. C. Olson, and B. A. Weitz. Chicago: American Marketing Association, 1982.

Belch, G. E. "Belief Systems and the Differential Role of the Self Concept." In *Advances in Consumer Research,* edited by H.K. Hunt. Ann Arbor, MI: Association for Consumer Research, 1978.

Belk, Sharyn S., and William E. Snell. Avoidance strategy use in intimate relationships. *Journal of Social and Clinical Psychology* Vol 7(1) (1988): 80-96.

Bellizzi, Joseph A., and Robert E. Hite. Supervising unethical salesforce behavior. *Journal of Marketing* Vol 53(2) (April 1989): 36-47.

Bengston, V. L., and M. C. Lovejoy. Values, Personality, and Social Structure. *American Behavioral Scientist.* No. 16 (July-August 1973): 880-912.

Berhman, Douglas N. and William D. Perreault, Jr. Measuring the performance of industrial salespersons. *Journal of Business Research* no. 10 (September 1982): 355-369.

Berlew, David E. How to increase your influence. *Training and Development Journal* Vol 39(9) (September 1985): 60-63.

Berkman, W.W. and C.C. Gilson. *Consumer Behavior: Concepts and Strategies.* Encino, CA: Dickenson Publishing, 1978.

Berry, N.C. Shifting Your Selling to Suit Changing Consumers. *Marketing Times* 28 (6) (November-December 1981): 9-10.

Berti, Anna E., Anna S. Bombi, and Rossana de Beni. Acquiring economic notions: Profit. *International Journal of Behavioral Development* Vol 9(1) (March 1986): 15-29.

Betz, Ellen L. Two tests of Maslow's theory of need fulfillment. *Journal of Vocational Behavior* Vol 24(2) (April 1984): 204-220.

Birnes, William, and Gary Markham. *Selling At The Top: The 100 Best Companies To Sell for In America.* New York: Harper & Row, 1985.

Bishop, Howard. *Portfolio of Ready-To-Use Model Sales Scripts.* Englewood Cliffs, NJ: Prentice Hall, 1989.

Bishop, William S., John L. Graham, and Michael H. Jones. Volatility of derived demand in industrial markets and its management implications. *Journal of Marketing* Vol 48(4) (Fall 1984): 95-103.

Bluen, Stephen D., Julian Barling, and Warren Burns. Predicting sales performance, job satisfaction, and depression by using the Achievement Strivings and Impatience-Irritability dimensions of Type A behavior. *Journal of Applied Psychology* Vol 75(2) (April 1990): 212-216.

Bond, Ronald N., Joan Welkowitz, Harlene Goldschmidt, and Sarah Wattenberg. Vocal frequency and person perception: .Effects of perceptual salience and nonverbal sensitivity. *Journal of Psycholinguistic Research* Vol 16(4) (July 1987): 335-350.

Bonoma, T.V., G. Zaltman, and W. J. Johnston. *Industrial Buying Behavior,* Cambridge, MA: Marketing Science Institute, 1977.

Boote, Alfred S. "An Exploratory Investigation of the Roles of Needs and Personal Values in the Theory of Buyer Behavior." PhD diss., Columbia University, 1975.

Boote, Alfred S. Market Segmentation by Personal Values and Salient Product Attributes. *Journal of Advertising Research* 21 (February 1981): 29-35.

Borresen, C. R. Decision making as a function of self and others. *Perceptual and Motor Skills* Vol 64(3, Pt 2) (June 1987): 1301-1302.

Boster, Franklin J., and James B. Stiff. Compliance-gaining message selection behavior. *Human Communication Research* Vol 10(4) (Summer 1984): 539-556.

Bottger, Preston C., and Irene K. Chew. The job characteristics model and growth satisfaction: Main effects of assimilation of work experience and context satisfaction. *Human Relations* Vol 39(6) (June 1986): 575-594.

Boyan, Lee. *Successful Cold Calling Selling.* New York: AMA BOOKS, 1989.

Bozinoff, L., and R. Cohen. "The Effects of Personal Values and Usage Situations on Product Attribute Importance." In *An Assessment of Marketing Thought and Practice,* edited by B. J. Walker, W. O. Bearden, W. R. Darden, P. E. Murphy, J. R. Nevin, J. C. Olson, and B. A. Weitz. Chicago: American Marketing Association, 1982.

Brent, John S., and Douglas E.Chismar. Person-centered apologetics: An empathic approach. *Journal of Psychology and Christianity* Vol 3(1) (Spring 1984): 18-26.

Broadbent, Simon, and Stephen Colman. Advertising effectiveness: Across brands. *Journal of the Market Research Society* Vol 28(1) (January 1986): 15-24.

Brooks, Michael. *Instant Rapport.* New York: Warner Books, 1989.

Brooks, Michael. *The Power of Business Rapport.* New York: Harper Collins, 1991.

Brown, M. S. Values--A Necessary but Neglected Ingredient of Motivation on the Job. *Academy of Management Review* 1 (1976): 15-23.

Brucks, Merrie, Gary M. Armstrong, and Marvin E. Goldberg. Children's use of cognitive defenses against television advertising: A cognitive response approach. *Journal of Consumer Research* Vol 14(4) (March 1988): 471-482.

Buckner, Michael, Naomi M. Meara, Edward J. Reese, and Maryann Reese. Eye movement as an indicator of sensory components in thought. *Journal of Counseling Psychology* Vol 34(3) (July 1987): 283-287.

Buller, David B. Distraction during persuasive communication: A meta-analytic review. *Communication Monographs* Vol 53(2) (June 1986): 91-114.

Bunn, M. D. Taxonomy of buying decision approaches. *Journal of Marketing* Vol. 57 (1993): 38-56.

Burger, Jerry M. Increasing compliance by improving the deal: The that's-not-all technique. *Journal of Personality and Social Psychology* Vol 51(2) (August 1986): 277-283.

Burger, Jerry M., and Robert A. Vartabedian. Public self-disclosure and speaker persuasiveness. *Journal of Applied Social Psychology* Vol 15(2) (1985): 153-165.

Burgoon, Michael, James P. Dillard, and Noel E. Doran. Friendly or unfriendly persuasion: The effects of violations of expectations by males and females. *Human Communication Research* Vol 10(2) (Winter 1983): 283-294.

Burleson, Brant R., and Wendy Samter. Effects of cognitive complexity on the perceived importance of communication skills in friends. *Communication Research* Vol 17(2) (April 1990): 165-182.

Bush, Robert P., Alan J. Bush, David J. Ortinau, and Joseph F. Hair. Developing a behavior-based scale to assess retail salesperson performance. *Journal of Retailing* Vol 66(1) (Spring 1990): 119-136.

Buzan, Tony. *Use Both Sides of Your Brain.* New York: Warner, 1977.

Buzan, Tony. *Make The Most of Your Mind.* New York: Linden Press, 1977.

Buzzotta, Victor, R. E. Lefton, and Manuel Sherberg. *Effective Selling Through Psychology.* Cambridge MA: Ballinger Publishing Company, 1982.

Caballero, Marjorie J., James R. Lumpkin, and Charles S. Madden. Using physical attractiveness as an advertising tool: An empirical test of the attraction phenomenon. *Journal of Advertising Research* Vol 29(4) (August-September 1989): 16-22.

Caballero, Marjorie J., and Paul J. Solomon. Effects of model attractiveness on sales response. *Journal of Advertising* Vol 13(1) (1984): 17-23, 33.

Cacioppo, John T., Richard E. Petty, Chuan Feng Kao, and Regina Rodriguez. Central and peripheral routes to persuasion: An individual difference perspective. *Journal of Personality and Social Psychology* Vol 51(5) (November 1986): 1032-1043.

Cantrill, James G., and David R. Seibold. The perceptual contrast explanation of sequential request strategy effectiveness. *Human Communication Research* Vol 13(2) (Winter 1986): 253-267.

Carman, J. M. "Values and Consumption Patterns: A Closed Loop." In *Advances in Consumer Research* V, edited by H.K. Hunt. Ann Arbor, MI: Association for Consumer Research 13 (1976), 1978.

Carrier, Michael R., Anthony T. Dalessio, and Steven H. Brown. Correspondence between estimates of content and criterion related validity values. *Personnel Psychology* Vol 43(1) (Spring 1990): 85-100.

Case, Thomas, Lloyd Dosier, Gene Murkison, and Bernard Keys. How managers influence superiors: A study of upward influence tactics. *Leadership and Organization Development Journal* Vol 9(4) (1988): 25-31.

Castleberry, Stephen B., A. S. Ehrenberg, and William H. Motes. Extended sales tests of product quality. *Journal of the Market Research Society* Vol 29(1) (January 1987): 3-14.

Chebat, Jean Charles, Pierre Filiatrault, Michel Laroche, and Catherine Watson. Compensatory effects of cognitive characteristics of the source, the message, and the receiver upon attitude change. *Journal of Psychology* Vol 122(6) (November 1988): 609-621.

Chebat, Jean Charles, and Jacques Picard. Receivers' self acceptance and the effectiveness of two-sided messages. *Journal of Social Psychology* Vol 128(3) (June 1988): 353-362.

Childs, Auralee, and Richard J. Klimoski. Successfully predicting career success: An application of the biographical inventory. *Journal of Applied Psychology* Vol 71(1) (February 1986): 3-8.

Christensen, J.A. Generational Value Differences. *The Gerontologist* 17 (1977): 367-374.

Chomsky, Noam. *Aspects of The Theory of Syntax.* Cambridge, MA: Massachussetts Institue of Technology Press, 1965.

Chomsky, Noam. *Knowledge of Language.* New York: Praeger Publishers, 1986.

Churchill, Gilbert A., and Anthony Pecotich. A structural equation investigation of the pay satisfaction-valence relationship among salespeople. *Journal of Marketing* Vol 46(4) (Fall 1982): 114-124.

Churchill, Gilbert A., Jr. A Paradigm for Developing Better Measures of Marketing Constructs. *Journal of Marketing Research* 16 (February 1979): 64-73.

Cialdini, Robert B. Influence: Science and practice (3rd ed.). New York: HarperCollins College Publishers, 1993.

Cialdini, Robert B., and Brad J. Sagarin. *Principles of Interpersonal Influence. Persuasion: Psychological Insights and Perspectives,* 2nd ed. Thousand Oaks, CA: Sage Publications, Inc., 2005.

Clare, D. A., and D. G. Sanford. Mapping Personal Value Space: A Study of Managers in Four Organizations. *Human Relations* 32 (1979): 659-666.

Clawson, C. J., and D. E. Vinson. "Human Values: An Historical and Interdisciplinary Analysis." In *Contributions to Consumer Research* V, Edited by H.K. Hunt, 396-402. Chicago: Association for Consumer Research (Proceedings), 1978.

Cody, Michael J., Mary L. Woelfel, and William J. Jordan. Dimensions of compliance gaining situations. *Human Communication Research* Vol 9(2) (Winter 1983): 99-113.

Colman, Stephen, and Gordon Brown. Advertising tracking studies and sales effects. *Journal of the Market Research Society* Vol 25(2) (April 1983): 165-183.

Comer, James M. Machiavellianism and inner vs outer directedness: A study of sales managers. *Psychological Reports* Vol 56(1) (February 1985): 81-82.

Comer, James M., Karen A. Machleit, and Rosemary R. Lagace. Psychometric assessment of a reduced version of INDSALES. *Journal of Business Research* Vol 18(4) (June 1989): 291-302.

Connell, H. Stanley. NLP techniques for salespeople. *Training and Development Journal* Vol 38(11) November 1984): 44-46.

Cooper, Joel, and Robert T. Croyle. Attitudes and attitude change. *Annual Review of Psychology* Vol 35 (1984): 395-426.

Cox, Anthony D., and John O. Summers. Heuristics and biases in the intuitive projection of retail sales. *Journal of Marketing Research* Vol 24(3) (August 1987): 290-297.

Cron, William L., Alan J. Dubinsky, and Ronald E. Michaels. The influence of career stages on components of salesperson motivation. *Journal of Marketing* Vol 52(1) (January 1988): 78-92.

Crosby, Lawrence A., James D. Gill, and Robert Lee. Life Status and Age as Surrogate Predictors of Value Orientation. Paper presented at the *Personal Values and Consumer Behavior Workshop,* University of Mississippi, 1983.

Crosby, Lawrence A., Kenneth R. Evans, and Deborah Cowles. Relationship quality in services selling: An interpersonal influence perspective. *Journal of Marketing* 54(3) (July 1990): 68-81.

Curtis, John M. Motivational techniques for individual and group psychotherapy. *Psychological Reports* Vol 54(1) (Februrary 1984): 271-277.

Danesi, Marcel. Visual metaphors: Psycholinguistic aspects. *Interfaces* Vol 12(1) (March 1985): 20-29.

Darden, D., W. Darden, and M. Carlson. *Social Class and Values.* Paper presented to the Mid-South Sociological Association, 1980.

Davis, Susan L., and Donald I. Davis. Neuro-Linguistic Programming and family therapy. *Journal of Marital and Family Therapy* Vol 9(3) (July 1983): 283-291.

Davis, Barbara Price, and Eric S. Knowles. A disrupt-then-reframe technique of social influence. *Journal of Personality and Social Psychology.* 76(2) (February 1999): 192-199.

Davison, W. Phillips. The third person effect in communication. *Public Opinion Quarterly* Vol 47(1) (Spring 1983): 1-15.

DeBono, Kenneth G. Investigating the social-adjustive and value-expressive functions of attitudes: Implications for persuasion processes. *Journal of Personality and Social Psychology* Vol 52(2) (February 1987): 279-287.

de Meuse, Kenneth P. A review of the effects of non-verbal cues on the performance appraisal process. *Journal of Occupational Psychology* Vol 60(3) (1987): 207-226.

DePaulo, Peter J. Research on deception in marketing communications: Its relevance to the study of non-verbal behavior. Special Issue: Deception. *Journal of Non-verbal Behavior* Vol 12(4, Pt 2) (Winter 1988): 253-273.

De Rose, Louis. *Value Selling.* New York: AMA BOOKS, 1989.

de Saussure, Ferdinand. *Course in General Linguistics.* La Salle, IL: Open Court Publishing, 1972.

DeTurck, Mark A. A transactional analysis of compliance-gaining behavior: Effects of noncompliance, relational contexts, and actors' gender. *Human Communication Research* Vol 12(1) (Fall 1985): 54-78.

Debevec, Kathleen, and Jerome B. Kernan. Self-referencing as a mediator of the physical attractiveness stereotype. *Genetic, Social, and General Psychology Monographs* Vol 113(4) (November 1987): 433-460.

Deese, James. The science of language and psychology. *Journal of Social Behavior and Personality* Vol 4(3) (1989): 203-208.

Demby, Emanuel H. Don't Count on Dissatisfied Customers to Make the Switch. *Marketing News* 22(2) (January 1988): 4-6.

Demirdjian, Z. S. Sales effectiveness of comparative advertising: An experimental field investigation. *Journal of Consumer Research* Vol 10(3) (December 1983): 362-364.

Dichter, E. *Handbook of Consumer Motivations:* The Psychology of the World of Objects. New York: McGraw-Hill, 1964.

Dickson, Peter R. Person-Situation: Segmentation's Missing Link. *Journal of Marketing* 46 (Fall 1983): 61.

Dillard, James P., and Michael Burgoon. Situational influences on the selection of compliance-gaining messages: Two tests of the predictive utility of the Cody-McLaughlin typology. *Communication Monographs* Vol 52(4) (December 1985): 289-304.

Dion, Paul A. Sales objections as a negotiation tactic. *Journal of Behavioral Economics* Vol 16(1) (Spring 1987): 33-47.

Dolgin, Kim G., and John Sabini. Experimental manipulation of a human non-verbal display: The tongue-show affects an observer's willingness to interact. *Animal Behaviour* Vol 30(3) (August 1982): 935-936.

Dorn, Fred J. Assessing Primary Representational System (PRS) preference for Neurolinguistic Programming (NLP) using three methods. *Counselor Education and Supervision* Vol 23(2) (December 1983): 149-156.

Drake, Roger A., and Brad R. Bingham. Induced lateral orientation and persuasibility. *Brain and Cognition* Vol 4(2) (April 1985): 156-164.

Dubinsky, Alan J., Steven W. Hartley, and Francis J. Yammarino., Boundary spanners and self-monitoring: An extended view. Psychological Reports Vol 57(1) (August 1985): 287-294.

Dubinsky, Alan J., and Michael Levy. Influence of organizational fairness on work outcomes of retail salespeople. *Journal of Retailing* Vol 65(2) (Summer 1989): 221-252.

Dubinsky, Alan J., and Steven J. Skinner. Job status and employees' responses: Effects of demographic characteristics. *Psychological Reports* Vol 55(1) (August 1984): 323-328.

Dubinsky, Alan J., and Francis J. Yammarino. Differential impact of role conflict and ambiguity on selected correlates: A two-sample test. *Psychological Reports* Vol 55(3) (December 1984): 699-707.

Edinger, Joyce A., and Miles L. Patterson. Nonverbal involvement and social control. *Psychological Bulletin* Vol 93(1) (January 1983): 30-56.

Einspruch, Eric L., and Bruce D. Forman. Observations concerning research literature on neuro-linguistic programming. *Journal of Counseling Psychology* Vol 32(4) (October1985): 589-596.

Elgin, Suzette. *Success With The Gentle Art of Verbal Self-Defense.* Englewood Cliffs, NJ: Prentice Hall, 1989.

Ellickson, Judy L. Representational systems and eye movements in an interview. *Journal of Counseling Psychology* Vol 30(3) (July 1983): 339-345.

Engel, J. F., and R. D. Blackwell. *Consumer Behavior.* Hinsdale, IL: The Dryden Press, 1982.

England, G. W. Personal Values Systems of American Managers. *Academy of Management Journal* 10 (1967): 53-68.

England, G. W., and R. Lee. The Relationship Between Managerial Values and Managerial Success in the United States, Japan, India, and Austrlia. *Journal of Applied Psychology* 59 (1974): 411-419.

Ettenson, Richard, and Janet Wagner. Retail buyers' saleability judgments: A comparison of information use across three levels of experience. *Journal of Retailing* Vol 62(1) (Spring 1986): 41-63.

Evans, Mary K., and Joseph H. Blase. Moral Perspectives of Life Insurance Sales Personnel: The Role of Organizational Culture in Selling Services. *International Studies of Management & Organization* 16 (Spring 1986): 80-94.

Farber, Edward D., and Jack A. Joseph. Factors in interview training. *Psychological Reports* Vol 57(3, Pt 1) (December 1985): 1021-1022.

Ferber, R. C. The Use of Operations Research Techniques is a Comprehensive Approach to Problem Solving in Sales Territory Management. *Industrial Marketing* (November 1981): 66-68.

Fern, Edward F., Kent B. Monroe, and Ramon A. Avila. Effectiveness of multiple request strategies: A synthesis of research results. *Journal of Marketing Research* Vol 23(2) (May 1986): 144-152.

Fidel, Stanley Leo. *Start Up Telemarketing.* New York: John Wiley & Sons, 1987.

Fishbein, Martin, and Rense Lange. The effects of crossing the midpoint on belief change: A replication and extension. *Personality and Social Psychology Bulletin* Vol 16(2) (June 1990): 189-199.

Flynn, Brian H. The Challenge of Multinational Sales Training. *Training & Development* Journal 41 (November 1987): 54-56.

Folkes, Valerie S., and Barbara Kotsos. Buyers' and sellers' explanations for product failure: Who done it? *Journal of Marketing* Vol 50(2) (April 1986): 74-80.

Fortin, P. A., and J. R. B. Ritchie. Influence structure in organizational buying behavior. *Journal of Business* Research Vol. 8 (1980): 277-299.

Foss, Donald J. Experimental psycholinguistics. *Annual Review of Psychology* Vol 39 (1988): 301-348.

Fowles, Jib. *Mass Advertising as Social Forecast:* A Method for Futures Research. Westport, CT: Greenwood Press, 1976.

Fox, Bonnie J. Selling the mechanized household: 70 years of ads in Ladies Home Journal. *Gender and Society* Vol 4(1) (March 1990): 25-40.

Fox, Derwin. The internal sale. *Training and Development Journal* Vol 40(9) (September 1986): 28-30.

Fraser, Cynthia, Robert E. Hite, and Paul L. Sauer. Increasing contributions in solicitation campaigns: The use of large and small anchorpoints. *Journal of Consumer Research* Vol 15(2) (September 1988): 284-287.

Freedman, Robert J. Compensation: Putting Salary Management to Work On the Sales Force. *Sales & Marketing Management* Vol 140 (9) (July 1988): 74-78.

Freedman, Jonathan L., John A. Cunningham, and Kirsten Krismer. Inferred values and the reverse-incentive effect in induced compliance. *Journal of Personality and Social Psychology* Vol 62(3) (March 1992): 357-368.

Frenzen, Jonathan K., and Harry L. Davis. Purchasing behavior in embedded markets. *Journal of Consumer Research* Vol 17(1) (June 1990): 1-12.

Friedrich, James. Learning to view psychology as a science: Self-persuasion through writing. Special Issue: Psychologists teach writing. *Teaching of Psychology* Vol 17(1) (February 1990): 23-27.

Fry, William R., Ira J. Firestone, and David L. Williams. Negotiation process and outcome of stranger dyads and dating couples: Do lovers lose? *Basic and Applied Social Psychology* Vol 4(1) (March 1983): 1-6.

Fukada, Hiromi. Effects of fear-arousing communications on resistance to subsequent counter-propaganda. *Japanese Journal of Experimental Social Psychology* Vol 27(2) (February 1988): 149-156.

Fullerton, Sammy D. "An Investigation of the Indirect Relationship Between Psychographics and Buyer Behavior." PhD diss., Michigan State University, 1988.

Furse, David H., Girish N. Punj, and David W. Stewart. A typology of individual search strategies among purchasers of new automobiles. *Journal of Consumer Research* Vol 10(4) (March 1984): 417-431.

Galinat, Withold H., and Gunther F. Muller. Verbal responses to different bargaining strategies: A content analysis of real-life buyer-seller interaction. *Journal of Applied Social Psychology* Vol 18(2) (February 1988): 160-178.

Garland, Howard, and Jane H. Adkinson. Standards, persuasion, and performance: A test of cognitive mediation theory. *Group and Organization
Studies* Vol 12(2) (June 1987): 208-220.

Gaski, John F. Interrelations among a channel entity's power sources: Impact of
the exercise of reward and coercion on expert, referent, and legitimate
power sources. *Journal of Marketing Research* Vol 23(1) (February
1986): 62-77.

Gatignon, Hubert, and Dominique M. Hanssens. Modeling marketing interactions
with application to salesforce effectiveness. *Journal of Marketing
Research* Vol 24(3) (August 1987): 247-257.

Geronilla, Linda. Neuro linguistic programming compared to reality therapy.
Journal of Reality Therapy Vol 9(1) (Fall 1989): 13-19.

Gfeller, Jeffrey D., Steven J. Lynn, and W. Eric Pribble. Enhancing hypnotic
susceptibility: Interpersonal and rapport factors. *Journal of Personality
and Social Psychology* Vol 52(3) (March 1987): 586-595.

Ghingold, M. Testing the 'buygrid' buying process model. *Journal of Purchasing
and Materials Management* Vol 22 (1986): 30-36.

Gibbs, Raymond W. On the psycholinguistics of sarcasm. *Journal of
Experimental Psychology General* Vol 115(1) (March 1986): 3-15.

Gibbs, Raymond W., and Richard J. Gerrig. How context makes metaphor
comprehension seem 'special. Special Issue: Context and metaphor
comprehension. *Metaphor and Symbolic Activity* Vol 4(3) (1989):
145-158.

Gibson, Lawrence D. 'Not recall.' *Journal of Advertising Research* Vol 23(1)
(February-March 1983): 39-46.

Glynn, Shawn M., Bruce K. Britton, K. Denis Muth, and Nukhet Dogan. Writing
and revising persuasive documents: Cognitive demands. *Journal of
Educational Psychology* Vol 74(4) (August 1982): 557-567.

Goldman, Morton, Odette Kiyohara, and Dorothy A. Pfannensteil. Interpersonal
touch, social labeling, and the foot-in-the-door effect. *Journal of Social
Psychology* Vol 125(2) (April 1985): 143-147.

Gonzales, Marti H., Elliot Aronson, and Mark A. Costanzo. Using social cognition
and persuasion to promote energy conservation: A quasi-experiment.
Journal of Applied Social Psychology Vol 18(12, Pt 2) (September 1988):
1049-1066.

Graham, John L., Dong Ki Kim, Chi Yuan Lin, and Michael Robinson. Buyer-seller negotiations around the Pacific Rim: Differences in fundamental exchange processes. *Journal of Consumer Research* Vol 15(1) June 1988): 48-54.

Greyser, Stephen. Advertising: Attacks and Counters. Harvard Business Review 50 (March 1972): 22-28.

Grinder, John, and Michael McMasters. *Precision.* Bonny Dune, CA: Precision Models, 1980.

Grinder, John, and Richard Bandler. *The Structure of Magic I & II.* Palo Alto, CA: Science & Behavior Books, 1976.

Gronhaug, Kjell, and Knut O. Ims. Setting the sales budget: An exploratory study. *Journal of Behavioral Decision Making* Vol 1(3) (July-September 1988): 177-186.

Gruner, Charles R. Prior attitude and perception of satirical theses. *Perceptual and Motor Skills* Vol 67(2) (October 1988): 677-678.

Gupta, Sunil. Impact of sales promotions on when, what, and how much to buy. *Journal of Marketing Research* Vol 25(4) (November 1988): 342-355.

Guth, W. D., and R. Tagiuri. Personal Values and Corporate Strategies. *Harvard Business Review* 43 (1965): 123-132.

Guttman, Jonathan. A Means-End Chain Model Based on Consumer Categoriztion Process. *Journal of Marketing* 46 (1982): 60-72.

Haley, R. I. Benefit Segmentation: A Decision Oriented Research Tool. *Journal of Marketing* 32 (July 1968): 30-35.

Haley, Russell I., Jack Richardson, and Beth M. Baldwin. The effects of nonverbal communications in television advertising. *Journal of Advertising Research* Vol 24(4) (August-September 1984): 11-18.

Hanan, Mack. *Consultative Selling.* New York: AMA BOOKS, 1970, 1995.

Hanan, Mack. *Key Account Selling.* New York: AMA BOOKS, 1982.

Hanel, Frank, Garry L. Martin, and Sandra Koop. Field testing of a self-instructional time management manual with managerial staff in an institutional setting. *Journal of Organizational Behavior Management* Vol 4(3-4) (Fall-Winter 1982): 81-96.

Hardy, Kenneth G. Key success factors for manufacturer's sales promotions in package goods. *Journal of Marketing* Vol 50(3) (July 1986): 13-23.

Haskell, Robert E. Empirical structures of mind: Cognition, linguistics, and transformation. *Journal of Mind and Behavior* Vol 5(1) (Winter 1984): 29-48.

Hawkins, D., R. Best, and K. Coney. *Consumer Behavior: Implications for Marketing Strategy*, 2d. ed. Dallas: Business Publications, 1983.

Hayakawa, S.E. "Poetry and Advertising." In *Language in Thought and Action*, 262-277. New York: Harcourt, Brace and World, 1964..

Hayakawa, S.I., and Alan Hayakawa. *Language In Thought And Action*. New York: Harcourt Brace Jovanovich, 5th Edition, 1990.

Hazleton, Vincent, William R. Cupach, and Jo Liska. Message style: An investigation of the perceived characteristics of persuasive messages. *Journal of Social Behavior and Personality* Vol 1(4) (October 1986): 565-574.

Heller, Robert. *The Super-Marketers*. New York: Truman Tally Books, 1987.

Helmstetter, Shad. *What To Say When You Talk To Your Self*. Scottsdale, AZ: Grindle Press, 1986.

Henry, Porter J. *Secrets Of The Master Sellers*. New York: AMA BOOKS, 1987.

Henry, W. A. Cultural Values Do Correlate with Consumer Discontent. *Journal of Marketing Research* 13 (1967): 121-132.

Herrmann, Ned. *The Creative Brain*. Lake Lure, North Carolina: Brain Books, 1988.

Heslin, Richard, and Patricia M. Sommers. The sleeper effect: Susceptibility of selective avoiders who hold extreme views. *Psychological Reports* Vol 61(3) (December 1987): 982.

Hinds, Pamela J. The curse of expertise: The effects of expertise and debiasing methods on prediction of novice performance. *Journal of Experimental Psychology:Applied* 5(2) (June 1999): 205-221.

Hinsz, Verlin B., and James H. Davis. Persuasive arguments theory, group polarization, and choice shifts. *Personality and Social Psychology Bulletin* Vol 10(2) (June 1984): 260-268.

Hoffman, Robert R. Recent psycholinguistic research on figurative language. *Annals of the New York Academy of Sciences* Vol 433 (December 1984): 137-166.

Hollen, Charles C. "The Stability of Values and Value System." Master's thesis, Michigan State University, 1967.

Hollenbeck, John R., and Charles R. Williams. Goal importance, self-focus, and the goal-setting process. *Journal of Applied Psychology* Vol 72(2) (May 1987): 204-211.

Hooper, Michael. The motivational bases of political behavior: A new concept and measurement procedure. *Public Opinion Quarterly* Vol 47(4) (Winter 1983): 497-515.

Howard, J. A., and J. N. Sheth. *The Theory of Buyer Behavior.* New York: John Wiley & Sons, Inc., 1969.

Howard, J. A. *Consumer Behavior: Application and Theory.* New York: McGraw-Hill Book Company, 1977.

Howell, Roy D., Danny N. Bellenger, and James B. Wilcox. Self-esteem, role stress, and job satisfaction among marketing managers. *Journal of Business Research* Vol 15(1) (February 1987): 71-84.

Humphrey, Stephen E., Aleksander P. J. Ellis, Donald E. Conlon, and Catherine H. Tinsley. Understanding Customer Reactions to Brokered Ultimatums: Applying Negotiation and Justice Theory. *Journal of Applied Psychology.* 89(3) (June 2004): 466-482.

Hunter, John E., and Franklin J. Boster. A model of compliance-gaining message selection. *Communication Monographs* Vol 54(1) (March 1987): 63-84.

Hunter, Lewis. *A Question of Values: Six Ways We Make the Personal Choices That Shape Our Lives.* San Francisco, CA: Harper & Row, 1990.

Ingram, Thomas N., and Danny N. Bellenger. Personal and organizational variables: Their relative effect on reward valences of industrial salespeople. *Journal of Marketing Research* Vol 20(2) (May 1983): 198-205.

Ingrasci, Hugh J. How to Reach Buyers in their Psychological Comfort Zone. *Industrial Marketing* 66 (July 1981): 60-64.

Jackson, R. G. A Preliminary Bicultural Study of Value Orientations and Leisure Attitudes. *Journal of Leisure Research* 5 (1973): 10-22.

Jacobs, Laurence, Reginald Worthley, and Charles Keown. Perceived buyer satisfaction and selling pressure versus pricing policy: A comparative study of retailers in ten developing countries. *Journal of Business Research* Vol 12(1) (March 1984): 63-74.

Jay, Timothy. The role of obscene speech in psychology. *Interfaces* Vol 12(3) (September 1985): 75-91.

Johnson, Blair T., and Alice H. Eagly. Involvement and persuasion: Types, traditions, and the evidence. *Psychological Bulletin* Vol 107(3) (May 1990): 375-384.

Johnson, C. Merle, and Roseann M. Masotti. Suggestive selling by waitstaff in family-style restaurants: An experiment and multisetting observations. *Journal of Organizational Behavior Management* 11(1) (1990): 35-54.

Johnson, MD, Spencer, and Larry Wilson. *The One Minute Sales* Person. New York: William Morrow and Company, Inc., 1984.

Johnston, Mark W., A. Parasuraman, and Charles M. Futrell. Extending a model of salesperson role perceptions and work-related attitudes: Impact of job tenure. *Journal of Business Research* Vol 18(4) (June 1989): 269-290.

Johnston, Mark W., A. Parasuraman, Charles M. Futrell, and Jeffrey Sager. Performance and job satisfaction effects on salesperson turnover: A replication and extension. *Journal of Business Research* Vol 16(1) (January 1988): 67-83.

Jowett, Garth S. Propaganda and communication: The re-emergence of a research tradition. *Journal of Communication* Vol 37(1) (Winter 1987): 97-114.

Jurik, Nancy C. Persuasion in a self-help group: Processes and consequences. *Small Group Behavior* Vol 18(3) (August 1987): 368-397.

Kamins, Michael A., and Lawrence J. Marks. Advertising puffery: The impact of using two-sided claims on product attitude and purchase intention. *Journal of Advertising* Vol 16(4) (1987): 6-15.

Kanter, D. L. "The Europeanizing of America: A Study in Changing Values." In *Advances in Consumer Research*, V, Edited by H. Keith Hunt, 408-410. Provo, Utah: Association for Consumer Research, 1978.

Kaplan, Martin F. A model of information integration in jury deliberation. *Academic Psychology Bulletin* Vol 5(1) (March 1983): 91-96.

Kapoor, Alka, Mahfooz A. Ansari, and Rashmi Shukla. Upward influence tactics as a function of locus of control and organizational context. *Psychological Studies* Vol 31(2) (July 1986): 190-199.

Kassarjian, H. H. Personality and Consumer Behavior: A Review. *Journal of Marketing Research 8* (November 1971): 409-418.

Kassarjian, H. H., and W. M. Kassarjian. Occupational Interests, Social Values, and Social Character. *Journal of Counseling Psychology* 12 (1966): 48-54.

Kassarjian, H. Content Analysis in Conumer Research. *Journal of Consumer Research* 4 (June 1977): 8-18.

Kean, Donald K., and Shawn M. Glynn. Writing persuasive documents: Audience considerations. *Journal of Instructional Psychology* Vol 14(1) (March 1987): 36-40.

Kelly, Michael H. Rhythm and language change in English. *Journal of Memory and Language* Vol 28(6) (December 1989): 690-710.

Keown, Charles F., and Ada L. Keown. Success factors for corporate woman executives. *Group and Organization Studies* Vol 7(4) (December 1982): 445-456.

Kerr, Barbara A., Charles D. Claiborn, and David N. Dixon. Training counselors in persuasion. *Counselor Education and Supervision* Vol 22(2) (December 1982): 138-148.

Key, Wilson Bryan. *Subliminal Seduction.* New York: Signet Books, 1972.

Killingmo, Bjorn. Beyond semantics: A clinical and theoretical study of isolation. *International Journal of Psycho Analysis* Vol 71(1) (1990): 113-126.

Kingstrom, Paul O., and Larry E. Mainstone. An investigation of the rater-ratee acquaintance and rater bias. *Academy of Management Journal* Vol 28(3) (September 1985): 641-653.

Kisielius, Jolita, and Brian Sternthal. Detecting and explaining vividness effects in attitudinal judgments. *Journal of Marketing Research* Vol 21(1) (February 1984): 54-64.

Kluckhohn, F. R., and R. L. Strodtbeck. *Variations in Value Orientations.* Evanston, Ill.: Row, Peterson and Co., 1961.

Kluchhohn, Clyde C. "The Study of Values." In *Values in America,* Edited by Donald N. Barrett. University of Notre Dame Press, 1961.

Knudsen, E. J. Selling Unseen Values. *American Salesman* 33 (September 1988): 9-13.

Kohli, Ajay K. Effects of supervisory behavior: The role of individual differences among salespeople. *Journal of Marketing* Vol 53(4) (October 1989): 40-50.

Kolczynski, Richard G. Meaning change miscues across four modes of writing. *Perceptual and Motor Skills* Vol 62(3) (June 1986): 753-754.

Korzybski, Alfred. *Science And Sanity.* Lakeville, CT: The International Non-Aristotelian Library Publishing Company, 1933.

Koseki, Yaeko. A study on factors inducing boomerang effects in persuasive communication: Concerning opinion discrepancy and forced commitment. *Japanese Journal of Psychology* Vol 54(1) (April 1983): 1-8.

Kothari, V. On Selling in Rome as Romans. *Marketing Times* Vol 25 (4) (July-August 1978): 23-24.

Krapfel, Robert E. Customer complaint and salesperson response: The effect of the communication source. *Journal of Retailing* Vol 64(2) (Summer 1988): 181-198.

Laborde, Genie. *Influencing With Integrity.* Palo Alto CA: Syntony Publishing, 1983.

Laborde, Genie. *Fine Tune Your Brain.* Palo Alto, CA: Syntony Publishing, 1988.

Lakoff, Robin Tolmach. *Talking Power.* New York: Basic Books, 1990.

Labounskaya, Vera A. Some developmental peculiarities of the ability for psychological interpretation of the non-verbal behaviour. *Voprosy Psikhologii* no. 3 (May-June 1987): 70-77.

Laird, A. W. Persuasion: A tool of courtroom communication. *Psychology A Quarterly Journal of Human Behavior* Vol 19(2-3) (1982): 50-57.

Lamude, Kevin G., and Allen Lichtenstein. The effects of motivational needs and rights situational dimension on compliance gaining strategies. *Communication Research Reports* Vol 2(1) (December 1985): 164-171.

LeVan, Elizabeth A. Nonverbal communication in the courtroom: Attorney beware. *Law and Psychology Review* Vol 8 (Spring 1984): 83-104.

Lee, Cynthia, and Dennis J. Gillen. Relationship of Type A behavior pattern, self-efficacy perceptions on sales performance. *Journal of Organizational Behavior* Vol 10(1) (January 1989): 75-81.

Lefton, Robert E., and Michael T. Hyatt. The professional sales training system. *Training and Development Journal* Vol 38(11) (November 1984): 35-37.

Leigh, Thomas W. and Arno J. Rethans. A Script Theoretic Analysis of Industrial Purchasing Behavior. *Journal of Marketing* no. 48 (Fall 1984): 22-32.

Leigh, Thomas W.and Patrick F. McGraw. Mapping the procedural knowledge of industrial sales personnel: A script-theoretic investigation. *Journal of Marketing* Vol 53(1) (January 1989): 16-34.

Leippe, Michael R., Anthony G. Greenwald, and Michael H. Baumgardner. Delayed persuasion as a consequence of associative interference: A context confusion effect. *Personality and Social Psychology Bulletin* Vol 8(4) (December 1982): 644-650.

Leong, Siew Meng, Paul S. Busch, and Deborah R. John. Knowledge bases and salesperson effectiveness: A script-theoretic analysis. *Journal of Marketing Research* Vol 26(2) (May 1989): 164-178.

Lessig, V. Parker. Measurement of Dependencies Between Values and Other levels of the Consumer's Belief Space. *Journal of Business Research* no. 83 (1976): 227-239.

Levitt, T. Marketing When Things Change. *Harvard Business Review* 55 (6) (November-December 1977): 107-113.

Lim, Chae Un, Alan J. Dubinsky, and Michael Levy. A psychometric assessment of a scale to measure organizational fairness. *Psychological Reports* Vol 63(1) (August 1988): 211-224.

Lindskold, Svenn, Gyuseog Han, and Brian Betz. The essential elements of communication in the GRIT strategy. *Personality and Social Psychology Bulletin* Vol 12(2) (June 1986): 179-186.

Lippman, Allen J. Sales training in the sales cycle. *Training and Development Journal* Vol 40(2) (February 1986): 56-61.

Lirtzman, Sidney I., and Avichai Shuv Ami. Credibility of sources of communication on products' safety hazards. *Psychological Reports*; Vol 58(3) (June 1986): 707-718.

Lucas, George H., A. Parasuraman, A., Robert A. Davis, and Ben M. Enis. An empirical study of salesforce turnover. *Journal of Marketing* Vol 51(3) (July 1987): 34-59.

Lui, Louisa, and Lionel G. Standing. Communicator credibility: Trustworthiness defeats expertness. *Social Behavior and Personality* Vol 17(2) (1989): 219-221.

Luthans, Fred, Robert Paul, and Lew Taylor. The impact of contingent reinforcement on retail salespersons' performance behaviors: A replicated field experiment. *Journal of Organizational Behavior-Management* Vol 7(1-2) (Spring-Summer 1985): 25-35.

Mackay, Harvey. *Swim With The Sharks.* New York: Ivy Books, 1989.

MacMurray, Bruce K., and Edward J. Lawler. Level-of-aspiration theory and initial stance in bargaining. *Representative Research in Social Psychology* Vol 16(1) (1986): 35-44.

MacDonald, Jerry P. "Reject the wicked man" coercive persuasion and deviance production: A study of conflict management. *Cultic Studies Journal* Vol 5(1) (1988): 59-121.

MacLachlan, James. Making a message memorable and persuasive. *Journal of Advertising Research* Vol 23(6) (December-January 1983-84): 51-59.

Mackie, Diane M. Systematic and nonsystematic processing of majority and minority persuasive communications. *Journal of Personality and Social Psychology* Vol 53(1) (July 1987): 41-52.

Mackie, Diane M., Leila T. Worth, and Arlene G. Asuncion. Processing of persuasive in-group messages. *Journal of Personality and Social Psychology* Vol 58(5) (May 1990): 812-822.

Maddux, James E., and Ronald W. Rogers. Protection motivation and self-efficacy: A revised theory of fear appeals and attitude change. *Journal of Experimental Social Psychology* Vol 19(5) (September 1983): 469-479.

Maheswaran, Durairaj, and Joan Meyers Levy. The influence of message framing and issue involvement. *Journal of Marketing Research* Vol 27(3) (August 1990): 361-367.

Mainstone, Larry E., and Dean M. Schroeder. Corporate hoop dreams: The power of metaphors in organizational transformation. *Consulting Psychology Journal: Practice and Research* Vol 51(3), (Summer 1999): 198-208.

Mallach, Efrem G. The truth about training for computer sales. *Training and Development Journal* Vol 40(11) (November 1986): 54-59.

Mankoff, A. W. Values--Not Attitudes--Are the Real Key to Motivation. *Management Review* 2 (1974): 23-24.

Manstead, Anthony S., H. L. Wagner, and C. J. MacDonald. Deceptive and nondeceptive communications: Sending experience, modality, and individual abilities. *Journal of Nonverbal Behavior* Vol 10(3) (Fall 1986): 147-167.

Marston, William Moulton. *Emotions of Normal People.* London: Kegan, Paul, Trench, Trubner and Co., Ltd., 1928.

Martin, Joanne, Philip Brickman, and Alan Murray. Moral outrage and pragmatism: Explanations for collective action. *Journal of Experimental Social Psychology* Vol 20(5) (September 1984): 484-496.

Martinko, Mark J. An O.B. Mod. analysis of consumer behavior. *Journal of Organizational Behavior Management* Vol 8(1) (Spring-Summer 1986): 19-43.

Marx, Gerry. How to sell your sales force on training. *Training and Development Journal* Vol 39(11) (November 1985): 49-50.

Maslow, Abraham H. *Motivation and Personality.* New York: Harper & Row, 1954.

Maslow, Abraham H. *Toward a Psychology of Being.* New York: Van Nostrand Reinhold, 1968.

Massey, M. *What You Are Is Where You Were When* (video program). Farmington Hills, MI: Magnetic Video Library, 1975.

Massey, M. *What You Are Is Where You See* (video program). Farmington Hills, MI: Magnetic Video Library, 1975.

Matteson, Michael T., John M. Ivancevich, and Samuel V. Smith. Relation of Type A behavior to performance and satisfaction among sales personnel. *Journal of Vocational Behavior* Vol 25(2) (October 1984): 203-214.

May, Rollo. *The Art of Counselling.* New York: Gardner Press, 1989.

McCall, Robert B., Thomas G. Gregory, and John P. Murray. Communicating developmental research results to the general public through television. *Developmental Psychology* Vol 20(1) (January 1984): 45-54.

McCracken, Grant, and Richard W. Pollay. Anthropological Analyses of Advertising. Working Paper #815, Faculty of Commerce, University of British Columbia: Vancouver, B.C., 1981.

McEnrue, Mary P. Length of experience and the performance of managers in the establishment phase of their careers. *Academy of Management Journal* Vol 31(1) (March 1988): 175-185.

McFarland, Richard G., Goutam N. Challagalla, and Tasadduq A. Shervani. Influence Tactics for Effective Adaptive Selling. *Journal of Marketing* Vol 70(4) (October 2006): 103-117.

McGuigan, F. J. How is linguistic memory accessed? A psychophysiological approach. *Pavlovian Journal of Biological Science* Vol 19(3) (July-September 1984): 119-136.

McIntyre, Shelby H., and Adrian B. Ryans. Task effects on decision quality in traveling salesperson problems. *Organizational Behavior and Human Performance* Vol 32(3) (December 1983): 344-369.

McMurray, N. N. Conflict in Human Values. *Harvard Business Review* 40 (1963): 130-145.

McNeill, Brian W., and Cal D. Stoltenberg. Reconceptualizing social influence in counseling: The Elaboration Likelihood Model. *Journal of Counseling Psychology* Vol 36(1) (January 1989): 24-33.

Meyer, Herbert H., and Michael S. Raich. An objective evaluation of a behavior modeling training program. *Personnel Psychology* Vol 36(4) (Winter 1983): 755-761.

Meyers, Renee A. Persuasive Arguments Theory: A test of assumptions. *Human Communication Research* Vol 15(3) (Spring 1989): 357-381.

Michaels, Ronald E., and Ralph L. Day. Measuring customer orientation of salespeople: A replication with industrial buyers. *Journal of Marketing Research* Vol 22(4) (November 1985): 443-446.

Milberg, Sandra, and Margaret S. Clark. Moods and compliance. Special Issue: The Social Context of Emotion. *British Journal of Social Psychology* Vol 27(1) (March 1988): 79-90.

Miller, Gerald R. On various ways of skinning symbolic cats: Recent research on persuasive message strategies. 2nd International Conference on Social Psychology and Language, Bristol, England 1983. *Journal of Language and Social Psychology* Vol 2(2-4) (1983): 123-140.

Miller, Lynn Carol, John H. Berg, and Richard L. Archer. Openers: Individuals Who Elicit Intimate Self-Disclosure. *Journal of Personality and Social Psychology* no. 44 (1983): 1253-1265.

Miller, Michael D., Rodney A. Reynolds, and Ronald E. Cambra. The influence of gender and culture on language intensity. *Communication Monographs* Vol 54(1) (March 1987): 101-105.

Miller, Robert, and Stephen Heiman. *Strategic Selling.* New York: Warner Books, 1985.

Miller, Robert, and Stephen Heiman. *Conceptual Selling.* Walnut Creek, CA: Miller-Heiman, Inc., 1987.

Mitchell, Arnold. *Consumer Values: A Typology.* Menlo Park, CA: SRI International, 1978.

Mitchell, Arnold. *Values: Scenarios for the 1980's.* Menlo Park, CA: SRI International, 1981.

Mitchell, Arnold. *The Integrateds.* Menlo Park, CA: SRI International, 1981.

Mitchell, Arnold. *Types of Achievers.* Menlo Park, CA: SRI International, 1981.

Moline, Kelsey L. What the Sales Culture is Not. *Bank Marketing* no. 21 (September 1989): 34-36.

Moncrief, William C. Selling activity and sales position taxonomies for industrial salesforces. *Journal of Marketing Research* Vol 23(3) (August 1986): 261-270.

Monguio Vecino, Ines, and Louis G. Lippman. Image formation as related to visual fixation point. *Journal of Mental Imagery* Vol 11(1) (Spring 1987): 87-96.

Moog, Carol. *Are They Selling Her Lips.* New York: William Morrow & Co., 1990.

Moore, Christopher W. The caucus: Private meetings that promote settlement. *Mediation Quarterly* no. 16 (Summer 1987): 87-101.

Moriarty, Mark M. Carryover effects of advertising on sales of durable goods. *Journal of Business Research* Vol 11(1) (March 1983): 127-137.

Morley, Donald D., and Kim B. Walker. The role of importance, novelty, and plausibility in producing belief change. *Communication Monographs* Vol 54(4) (December 1987): 436-442.

Moschis, George. *Consumer Socialization.* Lexington, MA: Lexington Books, 1987.

Motowidlo, Stephan J. Predicting sales turnover from pay satisfaction and expectation. *Journal of Applied Psychology* Vol 68(3) (August 1983): 484-489.

Mukhopadhyay, Indrani. Advertisement attributes for creating a favourable selling climate. *Vikalpa* Vol 8(1) (Januart-March 1983): 23-28.

Muller, Thomas E. Buyer response to variations in product information load. *Journal of Applied Psychology* Vol 69(2) (May 1984): 300-306.

Munch, James M., and John L. Swasy. Rhetorical question, summarization frequency, and argument strength effects on recall. *Journal of Consumer Research* Vol 15(1) (June 1988): 69-76.

Munson, J. M. An Investigation of Value Inventories for Applications to Cross-Cultural Marketing Research. *Proceedings of the American Institute of Decision Sciences* no. 1. (1977): 625-626.

Munson, J. M., and S. H. McIntyre. Developing Practical Procedures for the Measurement of Personal Values in Cross-Cultural Marketing. *Journal of Marketing Research* 16 (1979): 55-60.

Murphy, Sheila E. Selling your wares: The missing PT competency. *Performance and Instruction* Vol 26(7) (September 1987): 5-8.

Myers, David C., and Sidney A. Fine. Development of a methodology to obtain and assess applicant experiences for employment. *Public Personnel Management* Vol 14(1) (Spring 1985): 51-64.

Myers, J. H. Benefit Structure Analysis: A New Tool for Product Planning. *Journal of Marketing* no. 40 (October 1976): 23-32.

Myers, M. Scott. Who Are Your Motivated Workers? *Harvard Business Review* no. 40 (1963): 73-88.

Nebeker, Delbert M., and Brian M. Neuberger. Productivity improvement in a purchasing division: The impact of a performance contingent reward system. *Evaluation and Program Planning* Vol 8(2) (1985): 121-134.

Neslin, Scott A., and Leonard Greenhalgh. Nash's theory of cooperative games as a predictor of the outcomes of buyer-seller negotiations: An experiment in media purchasing. *Journal of Marketing Research* Vol 20(4) (November 1983): 368-379.

Netemeyer, Richard G., Mark W. Johnston, and Scot Burton. Analysis of role conflict and role ambiguity in a structural equations framework. *Journal of Applied Psychology* Vol 75(2) (April 1990): 148-157.

Neuliep, James W. Self-report vs. actual use of persuasive messages by high and low dogmatics. *Journal of Social Behavior and Personality* Vol 1(2) (April 1986): 213-222.

Newton, Deborah A., and Judee K. Burgoon. The use and consequences of verbal influence strategies during interpersonal disagreements. *Human Communication Research* Vol 16(4) (Summer 1990): 477-518.

O'Keefe, Barbara J., and Gregory J. Shepherd. The communication of identity during face-to-face persuasive interactions: Effects of perceiver's construct differentiation and target's message strategies. Special Issue: Social Cognition and *Communication. Communication Research* Vol 16(3) (June 1989): 375-404.

Oda, Masami. An analysis of relation between personality traits and job performance in sales occupations. *Japanese Journal of Psychology* Vol 53(5) (December 1982): 274-280.

Ohsawa, Takeshi. The employee selection in Japanese business industry. *Japanese Journal of Behaviormetrics* Vol 15(1) (September 1987): 53-59.

Oliver, Richard L. A Cognitive Model of Antecedents and Consequences of Consumer Satisfaction. *Journal of Marketing Research* no. 14 (November 1980): 460.

Oliver, Richard L., and John E. Swan. Consumer perceptions of interpersonal
equity and satisfaction in transactions: A field survey approach. *Journal
of Marketing* Vol 53(2) (April 1989): 21-35.

Olson, Carl W. Big Gun, No Bullets. *Successful Selling & Sales Management.*
September (1988) :1-4.

Orpen, Christopher. Patterned behavior description interviews versus unstruc-
tured interviews: A comparative validity study. *Journal of Applied
Psychology* Vol 70(4) (November 1985): 774-776.

Packard, Vance. *The Hidden Persuaders.* New York: Van Rees Press, 1957.

Pardini, Anton U., and Richard D. Katzev. Applying full-cycle social psychology
to consumer marketing: The defusing objections technique. *Journal of
Economic Psychology* Vol 7(1) (March 1986): 87-94.

Parsons, Talcott and Edward A. Shils. *Toward a General Theory of Action.*
Cambridge, MA: Harvard University Press, 1951.

Patch, Michael E. The role of source legitimacy in sequential request strategies
of compliance. *Personality and Social Psychology Bulletin* Vol 12(2)
(June 1986): 199-205.

Pauley, L. Lynn. Customer weight as a variable in salespersons' response time.
Journal of Social Psychology Vol 129(5) (October 1989): 713-714.

Pentony, Joseph F. Relationship between involvement in an issue and number of
arguments. *Psychological Reports* Vol 60(1) (February 1987): 219-226.

Perls, Fritz. *The Gestalt Approach: Eyewitness To Therapy.* Palo Alto, CA:
Science and Behavior Books, 1973.

Peterson, Lizette, and Katherine E. Lewis. Preventive intervention to improve
children's discrimination of the persuasive tactics in televised advertising. *Journal of Pediatric Psychology* Vol 13(2) (June 1988): 163-170.

Petty, Richard E., and John T. Cacioppo. Involvement and persuasion: Tradition
versus integration. *Psychological Bulletin* Vol 107(3) (May 1990): 367-374.

Petty, Richard E., John T. Cacioppo, Constantine Sedikides, and Alan J.
Strathman. Affect and persuasion: A contemporary perspective. Special
Issue: Communication and Affect. *American Behavioral Scientist* Vol
31(3) (January-February 1988): 355-371.

Petty, Richard E., et-al. The effects of recipient posture on persuasion: A cognitive response analysis. *Personality and Social Psychology Bulletin* Vol
9(2) (June 1983): 209-222.

Pittam, Jeffrey. The relationship between perceived persuasiveness of nasality and source characteristics for Australian and American listeners. *Journal of Social Psychology* Vol 130(1) (February 1990): 81-87.

Pitts, Robert E. "The Influence of Personal Value Systems on Product Class and Brand Preferences: A Segmentation Approach." PhD diss., University of South Carolina, 1977.

Pitts, Robert E. and Arch G. Woodside. Personal Value Influences on Consumer Product Class and Brand Preferences. *The Journal of Social Psychology* 119 (1983): 37-53.

Pitts, Robert, and Arch G. Woodside. *Personal Values and Consumer Psychology.* Lexington, MA: Lexington Books, 1984.

Plotkin, Harris M. What makes a successful salesperson? *Training and Development Journal* Vol 41(9) (September 1987): 54-56.

Posner, B. Z., and J. M. Munson. The Importance of Personal Values in Understanding Organizational Behavior. *Journal of Human Resource Management* no. 18 (1979): 9-14.

Prince, Alan, and Steven Pinker. Rules and connections in human language. *Trends in Neurosciences* Vol 11(5) (May 1988): 195-202.

Prus, Robert. Purchasing products for resale: Assessing suppliers as 'partners-in-trade.' *Symbolic Interaction* Vol 7(2) (Fall 1984): 249-278.

Puckett, James M., Richard E. Petty, John T. Cacioppo, and Donald L. Fischer. The relative impact of age and attractiveness stereotypes on persuasion. *Journal of Gerontology* Vol 38(3) (May 1983): 340-343.

Rackham, Neil. *SPIN Selling.* New York: McGraw-Hill, 1988.

Rafaeli, Anat. When clerks meet customers: A test of variables related to emotional expressions on the job. *Journal of Applied Psychology* Vol 74(3) (June 1989): 385-393.

Ralis, Michael T., and Richard M. O'Brien. Prompts, goal setting and feedback to increase suggestive selling. *Journal of Organizational Behavior Management* Vol 8(1) (Spring-Summer 1986): 5-18.

Rankin, Carol. Using empathy when dealing with change. *Issues in Radical Therapy* Vol 10(2) (Summer 1982): 30-32.

Reagan, Carmen C.and Duane I. Miller. A work commitment typology of sales representatives in the college textbook industry. Journal of Business and Psychology Vol 3(4) (Summer 1989): 459-464.

Reilly, Thomas P. *Value Added Selling Techniques*. St. Louis, MO: Motivation Press, 1987.

Reinard, John C. The empirical study of the persuasive effects of evidence: The status after fifty years of research. *Human Communication Research* Vol 15(1) (Fall 1988): 3-59.

Reynolds, T. J., and J. Gutman. "Laddering: Extending the Repertory Grid Methodology to Construct Attribute Consequence Value Hierarchies." Paper presented at Personal Values and Consumer Behavior Workshop, The University of Mississippi, Oxford, Mississippi, May 6-7, 1983.

Rhea, Marti J., and Tom K. Massey. Contrasting views of effectiveness in sales-promotion relationships. *Journal of Advertising Research* Vol 29(5) (October-November 1989): 49-56.

Rice, Berkeley. The selling of life-styles. *Psychology Today* Vol 22(3) (March 1988): 46-50.

Robberson, Margaret R., and Ronald W. Rogers. Beyond fear appeals: Negative and positive persuasive appeals to health and self-esteem. *Journal of Applied Social Psychology* Vol 18(3, Pt 1) (March 1988): 277-287.

Robinson, P. J., C. W. Faris, and Y. Wind. *Industrial Buying Behavior and Creative Marketing*. Boston, MA: Allyn & Bacon, 1967.

Roddy, Brian L., and Gina M. Garramone. Appeals and strategies of negative political advertising. *Journal of Broadcasting and Electronic Media* Vol 32(4) (Fall 1988): 415-427.

Rogers, Carl. *A Way of Being*. New York: Houghton Mifflin, 1980.

Rokeach, Milton. *Beliefs, Attitudes and Values*. San Francisco, CA: Jossey-Bass, 1969.

Rokeach, M. *The Nature of Human Values*. New York: Free Press, 1973.

Rokeach, M. *Understanding Human Values*: Individual and Societal. New York: Free Press, 1979.

Rousseau, Deon. A study on pre-purchase information search by consumers. *South African Journal of Psychology* Vol 12(1) (1982): 19-23.

Rule, Brendan G., Gay L. Bisanz, and Melinda Kohn. Anatomy of a persuasion schema: Targets, goals, and strategies. *Journal of Personality and Social Psychology* Vol 48(5) (May 1985): 1127-1140.

Sagarin, Brad J., Robert B. Cialdini, William E. Rice, and Sherman B. Serna. Dispelling the illusion of invulnerability: The motivations and mechanisms of resistance to persuasion. *Journal of Personality and Social Psychology* 83(3) (September 2002): 526-541.

Sagie, Abraham, Dov Elizur, and Charles W. Greenbaum. Job experience, persuasion strategy and resistance to change: An experimental study. *Journal of Occupational Behaviour* Vol 6(2) (April 1985): 157-162.

Sakaki, Hilobumi. Effects of communication discrepancy on opinion change and on evaluation change of source credibility: Analyses on conditions of boomerang effect arousal. *Japanese Journal of Experimental Social Psychology* Vol 24(1) (August 1984): 67-82.

Sanders, Keith R., and L. E. Atwood. "Value Change Initiated by Mass Media." At International Communication Association Convention, Berlin, Germany, June 1977.

Sawa, Sonja L., and Ghazi H. Sawa. The value confrontation approach to enduring behavior modification. *Journal of Social Psychology* Vol 128(2) (April 1988): 207-215.

Schiffman, Stephen. *Cold Calling Techniques.* Boston, MA: Bob Adams Press, 1982.

Schul, Patrick L., William M. Pride, and Taylor L. Little. The impact of channel leadership behavior on intra-channel conflict. *Journal of Marketing* Vol 47(3) (Summer 1983): 21-34.

Sheth, J. N. A model of industrial buyer behavior. *Journal of Marketing* Vol 37 (1973): 50-6.

Shulman, Richard E. Changing a Company's Focus from Buying to Selling. *Supermarket Business* 45(4) (April 1990): 13-14.

Schwarz, Norbert, Martin Kumpf, and Wolf Bussmann. Resistance to persuasion as a consequence of influence attempts in advertising and non-advertising communications. *Psychology A Quarterly Journal of Human Behavior* Vol 23(2-3) (1986): 72-76.

Schwarz, Norbert, Wofgang Servay, and Martin Kumpf. Attribution of arousal as a mediator of the effectiveness of fear-arousing communications. *Journal of Applied Social Psychology* Vol 15(2) (1985): 178-188.

Sciortino, John J., John H. Huston, and Roger W. Spencer. Risk and income distribution. *Journal of Economic Psychology* Vol 9(3) (September 1988): 399-408.

Scott, J. E., and L. H. Lamont. Relating Consumer Values to Consumer Behavior: A Model and Method for Investigation. *In Increasing Marketing Productivity*, edited by T. V. Greer, 283-288. Chicago: American Marketing Association, 1973.

Segal, Mary E., and Clark R. McCauley. The sociability of commercial exchange in rural, suburban, and urban locations: A test of the urban overload hypothesis. *Basic and Applied Social Psychology* Vol 7(2) (June 1986): 115-135.

Seldman, Marty. *Super Selling Through Self-Talk*. Los Angeles, CA: Price Stern and Sloan, Inc., 1988.

Shaffer, David R., Richard Reardon, E. Gil Clary, and Cyril J. Sadowski. The effects of information on perspectives and attitude change. *Journal of Social Psychology* Vol 117(1) (June 1982): 125-133.

Sharma, Arun. Consumer decision-making, salespeople's adaptive selling and retail performance. *Journal of Business Research* 54(2) (Nov 2001): 125-129.

Sharpless, Elizabeth A. Identity formation as reflected in the acquisition of person pronouns. *Journal of the American Psychoanalytic Association* Vol 33(4) (1985): 861-885.

Sharpley, Christopher F. Predicate matching in NLP: A review of research on the preferred representational system. *Journal of Counseling Psychology* Vol 31(2) (April 1984): 238-248.

Sherer, Mark, and Ronald W. Rogers. The role of vivid information in fear appeals and attitude change. *Journal of Research in Personality* Vol 18(3) (September 1984): 321-334.

Shook, Robert L. *Ten Greatest Salespersons*. New York: Barnes & Noble Books, 1980.

Simons, Ronald L. Inducement as an approach to exercising influence. *Social Work* Vol 30(1) (January-February 1985): 56-62.

Smith, J. Brock, and Donald W. Barclay. Selling partner relationships: The role of interdependence and relative influence. *Journal of Personal Selling & Sales Management* Vol 19(4) (Fall 1999): 21-40.

Smith, Mary J. Contingency rules theory, context, and compliance behaviors. *Human Communication Research* Vol 10(4) (Summer 1984): 489-512.

Soldow, Gary F., and Gloria P. Thomas. Relational communication: Form versus content in the sales interaction. *Journal of Marketing* Vol 48(1) (Winter 1984): 84-93.

Sorrentino, Richard M., D. Ramona Bobocel, Maria Z. Gitta, and James M. Olson, et al. Uncertainty orientation and persuasion: Individual differences in the effects of personal relevance on social judgments. *Journal of Personality and Social Psychology* Vol 55(3) (September 1988): 357-371.

Spence, Donald P. Narrative persuasion. *Psychoanalysis and Contemporary Thought* Vol 6(3) (1983): 457-481.

Spiro, Rosann L., William D. Perreault and Fred D. Reynolds. The Personal Selling Process: A Critical Review and Model. *Industrial Marketing Management* 5 (Spring 1976): 352-354.

Spiro, Rosann L., and Barton A. Weitz. Adaptive selling: Conceptualization, measurement, and nomological validity. *Journal of Marketing Research* Vol 27(1) (February 1990): 61-69.

Spiro, Rosann L., and William D. Perreault. Influence Used by Industrial Salespeople: Influence Strategy Mixes and Situational Determinants. *Journal of Business* 59 (July 1979): 435-455.

Sprowl, John P. Sales communication: An analysis of sex differences in compliance-gaining strategy use. *Communication Research Reports* Vol 3 (December 1986): 90-93.

Sprowl, John P., and Marshall Senk. Sales communication: Compliance-gaining strategy choice and sales success. *Communication Research Reports* Vol 3 (December 1986): 64-68.

Stewart, Lea P., William B. Gudykunst, Stella Ting Toomey, and Tsukasa Nishida. The effects of decision-making style on openness and satisfaction within Japanese organizations. *Communication Monographs* Vol 53(3) (September 1986): 236-251.

Stoltenberg, Cal D., Mark M. Leach, and Avery Bratt. The Elaboration Likelihood Model and psychotherapeutic persuasion. *Journal of Cognitive Psychotherapy* Vol 3(3) (Fall 1989): 181-199.

Strube, Michael J., and Carol M. Werner. Personal space claims as a function of interpersonal threat: The mediating role of need for control. *Journal of Nonverbal Behavior* Vol 8(3) (Spring 1984): 195-209.

Sujan, Harish, Mita Sujan, and James R. Bettman. Knowledge structure differences between more effective and less effective salespeople. *Journal of Marketing Research* Vol 25(1) (February 1988): 81-86.

Sullivan, Gary L. Music format effects in radio advertising. *Psychology and Marketing* Vol 7(2) (Summer 1990): 97-108.

Sutton, Robert I., and Anat Rafaeli. Untangling the relationship between displayed emotions and organizational sales: The case of convenience stores. *Academy of Management Journal* Vol 31(3) (September 1988): 461-487.

Swan, John E., David R. Rink, G. E. Kiser, and Warren S. Martin. Industrial buyer image of the saleswoman. *Journal of Marketing* Vol 48(1) (Winter 1984): 110-116.

Swaroff, Philip G.; Lizabeth A. Barclay, and Alan R. Bass. Recruiting sources: Another look. *Journal of Applied Psychology* Vol 70(4) (November 1985): 720-728.

Swasy, John L., and James M. Munch. Examining the target of receiver elaborations: Rhetorical question effects on source processing and persuasion. *Journal of Consumer Research* Vol 11(4) (March 1985): 877-886.

Sypher, Howard E., Beverly D. Sypher, and John W. Haas. Getting emotional: The role of affect in interpersonal communication. Special Issue: Communication and Affect. *American Behavioral Scientist* Vol 31(3) (January-February 1988): 372-383.

Szymanski, David M. Determinants of selling effectiveness: The importance of declarative knowledge to the personal selling concept. *Journal of Marketing* Vol 52(1) (January 1988): 64-77.

Tadlock, Dolores R. A practical application of psycholinguistics and Piaget's theory to reading instruction. *Reading Psychology* Vol 7(3) (1986): 183-195.

Tannen, Deborah. *That's Not What I Meant.* New York: William Morrow, Inc., 1986.

Tardy, Charles H., R. Joseph Childs, and Michael M. Hampton. Communication and Type A coronary-prone behavior: Preliminary studies of expressive and instrumental communication. *Perceptual and Motor Skills* Vol 61(2) (October 1985): 603-614.

Teas, R. Kenneth. Supervisory behavior, role stress, and the job satisfaction of industrial salespeople. *Journal of Marketing Research* Vol 20(1) (February 1983): 84-91.

Telenson, Paul A., Ralph A. Alexander, and Gerald V. Barrett. Scoring the biographical information blank: A comparison of three weighting techniques. *Applied Psychological Measurement* Vol 7(1) (Winter 1983): 73-80.

Trawick, I. Fredrick, John E. Swan, and David R. Rink. Back-door selling: Violation of cultural versus professional ethics by salespeople and purchaser choice of the supplier. Special Issue: Articles from the 1987 Southern Marketing Association Conference. *Journal of Business Research* Vol 17(3) (November 1988): 299-309.

Tyagi, Pradeep K. Relative importance of key job dimensions and leadership behaviors in motivating salesperson work performance. *Journal of Marketing* Vol 49(3) (Summer 1985): 76-86.

Vallacher, Robin R., Daniel M. Wegner, and Maria P. Somoza. That's easy for you to say: Action identification and speech fluency. *Journal of Personality and Social Psychology* Vol 56(2) (February 1989): 199-208.

Vidmar, Neil, and Nancy M. Laird. Adversary social roles: Their effects on witnesses' communication of evidence and the assessments of adjudicators. *Journal of Personality and Social Psychology* Vol 44(5) (May 1983): 888-898.

Vinson, D. E., and J. Gutman. "Personal Values and Consumer Discontent." *In Proceedings of the American Institute for Decision Sciences,* edited by R. J. Ebert, R. J. Monroe, and K .J. Roering, 201-203. November, 1978.

Vinson, D. E., J. M. Munson, and M. Nakanishi. An Investigation of the Rokeach Value Survey for Consumer Research Applications. In *Advances in Consumer Research,* edited by W. D. Perreault. Atlanta: Association for Consumer Research, 1977.

Vinson, D. E. "Human Values and the Marketing Function." In *Avoiding Social Catastrophes and Maximizing Social Opportunities: The General Systems Challenge,* edited by R. Erison. Washington,D.C.: Society for General Systems Research, 1978.

Wagner, Janet, Richard Ettenson, and Jean Parrish. Vendor selection among retail buyers: An analysis by merchandise division. *Journal of Retailing*, Vol 65(1) (Spring 1989): 58-79.

Walker, O. C., Jr., G. A. Churchill, Jr., and N. M. Ford. Motivation and
Performance in Industrial Selling: Existing Knowledge and Needed
Research. *Journal of Marketing Research* 14 (1977): 156-168.

Wall, Mark D.; Turdy Klecker, John H. Amendt, and R. DuRee Bryant.
Therapeutic compliments: Setting the stage for successful therapy.
Journal of Marital and Family Therapy Vol 15(2) (April 1989):
159-167.

Walsh, James P., Susan J. Ashford, and Thomas E. Hill. Feedback obstruction:
The influence of the information environment on employee turnover
intentions. *Human Relations* Vol 38(1) (January 1985): 23-46.

Wang, Theodore, Richard Brownstein, and Richar Katzev. Promoting charitable
behaviour with compliance techniques. *Applied Psychology - An
International Review* Vol 38(2) (April 1989): 165-183.

Waters, L. K., and Michael Collins. Effect of pricing conditions on preference
reversals by business students and managers. *Journal of Applied
Psychology* Vol 69(2) (May 1984): 346-348.

Watzlawick,Weakland and Fisch. *Change.* New York: W.W. Norton, 1974.

Week, W. A., and Lynn R. Kahle. Social Values and Salespeople's Effort:
Entrepreneurial Versus Routine Selling. *Journal of Business Research.*
20 (2) (March 1990): 183-190.

Weekley, Jeff A., and Joseph A. Gier. Reliability and validity of the situational
interview for a sales position. *Journal of Applied Psychology* Vol 72(3)
(August 1987): 484-487.

Weeks, William A., Lawrence B. Chonko, and Lynn R. Kahle. Performance
Congruence and Value Congruence Impact on Sales Force Annual Sales.
Journal of the Academy of Marketing Science 17 (Fall 1989): 345-352.

Weiss, Robert F., Michele K. Steigleder, Richard A. Feinberg, and Robert E.
Cramer. Classical conditioning of attitudes as a function of persuasion
trials and source consensus. *Bulletin of the Psychonomic Society* Vol
20(1) (July 1982): 21-22.

Weitz, Barton A. The Relationship Between Salesperson's Performance and
Understanding of Consumer Decision Making. *Journal of Marketing
Research* 15 (1978): 501-516.

Weitz, Barton A. Effectiveness of Sales Interactions: A Contingency Framework.
Journal of Marketing 45 (Winter 1981): 85-103.

Weitz, Barton A. "A Critical Review of Personal Selling Research: The Need For a Contingency Approach." In *Critical Issues in Sales Management: State-of-the-Art and Future Research Needs*. Edited by G. Albaum and G. Churchill. Eugene, OR: College of Business Administration, University of Oregon, 1979.

Wexler, P. J. Explanation by example. *Language and Communication* Vol 2(3) (1982): 303-309.

Wexley, Kenneth N., and Scott A. Snell. Managerial power: A neglected aspect of the performance appraisal interview. *Journal of Business Research*; Vol 15(1) (February 1987): 45-54.

Williams, M. Lee, and Nancy K. Untermeyer. Compliance-gaining strategies and communicator role: An analysis of strategy choices and persuasive efficacy. *Communication Research* Reports Vol 5(1) (June 1988): 10-18.

Wilner, Jack. Tending goals for sales management. *Training and Development Journal* Vol 39(11) (November 1985): 46-47.

Wise, Paula S., Gene F. Smith, and Frank E. Fulkerson. Occupations of psychology majors receiving undergraduate degrees from Western Illinois University. *Teaching of Psychology* Vol 10(1) (February 1983): 53-54.

Wilson, Larry. *Changing The Game: The New Way To Sell*. New York: Simon and Schuster, 1987.

Wood, Wendy,and Carl A. Kallgren. Communicator attributes and persuasion: Recipients' access to attitude-relevant information in memory. *Personality and Social Psychology Bulletin* Vol 14(1) (March 1988): 172-182.

Woodall, W. Gill, and Judee K. Burgoon. Talking fast and changing attitudes: A critique and clarification. *Journal of Nonverbal Behavior* Vol 8(2) (Winter 1983): 126-142.

Woodside, Arch G., amd Praveen K. Soni. Assessing the quality of advertising inquiries by mode of response. *Journal of Advertising Research* Vol 28(4) (August-September 1988): 31-37.

Wong, Y. H., T. K. P. Leung, Ricky Y. K. Chan, Chester K. M. To, Stanley H. F. So. Is Total Trust Possible?: An Empirical Study in Relationship Selling. *Journal of International Consumer Marketing* 16(4) (2004): 107-131.

Wright, Edward F., and Gary L. Wells. Is the attitude-attribution paradigm suitable for investigating the dispositional bias? *Personality and Social Psychology Bulletin* Vol 14(1) (March 1988): 183-190.

Yankelovich, D. *New Rules*. New York: Random House, 1981.

Yammarino, Francis J., and Alan J. Dubinsky. Salesperson performance and managerially controllable factors: An investigation of individual and work group effects. *Journal of Management* Vol 16(1) (March 1990): 87-106.

Yammarino, Francis J., Alan J. Dubinsky, and Steven W. Hartley. An approach for assessing individual versus group effects in performance evaluations. *Journal of Occupational Psychology* Vol 60(2) (June 1987): 157-167.

Yeh, Bijou Y., David Lester, and Deborah L. Tauber. Subjective stress and productivity in real estate sales people. *Psychological Reports* Vol 58(3) June 1986): 981-982.

Yinon, Yoel, and Michael Dovrat. The reciprocity-arousing potential of the requester's occupation, its status and the cost and urgency of the request as determinants of helping behavior. *Journal of Applied Social Psychology* Vol 17(4) (April 1987): 429-435.

Young, Louise, and Gerald Albaum. Measurement of trust in salesperson-customer relationships in direct selling. *Journal of Personal Selling & Sales Management* 23(3) (Summer 2003): 253-269.

ABOUT THE AUTHOR

Gregory Stebbins, Ed.D., has built an outstanding reputation in the fields of sales, sales management, and sales consulting over the last 30 years. He applies his extensive educational background in business and human motivation (MBA Finance from University of Southern California, Ed.D. from Pepperdine's School of Education & Psychology) to his hands-on, practical approach to sales and sales training. He developed the PeopleSavvy principles over years of research in interpersonal psychology tempered with over three decades of in-the-field work in sales. When he is not presenting PeopleSavvy seminars to sales leaders around the globe, Greg lives with his wife, Jennifer Cayer, in Marina del Rey, California.

Printed in the United States
71326LV00002B/112-510